Logic Pro

Tips and Tricks

Stephen Bennett

PC Publishing

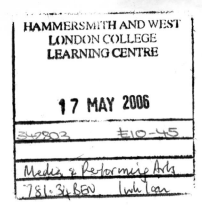
PC Publishing
Keeper's House
Merton
Thetford
Norfolk IP25 6QH
UK

Tel +44 (0)1953 889900
Fax +44 (0)1953 889901
email info@pc-publishing.com
website http://www.pc-publishing.com

First published 2006

ISBN 1 870775 333

British Library Cataloguing in Publication Data
A catalogue record for this book is available from the British Library

Cover design by Hilary Norman Design Ltd

Printed and bound in Great Britain by Biddles, Kings Lynn, Norfolk

Introduction

Apple's Logic audio sequencer program is highly renowned for its flexibility and customisable nature. Like any complex piece of software, the means to achieving a given goal is not always obvious – a problem compounded by Logic's ability to perform most functions in several different ways. Occasionally, Logic's features are obscure and poorly documented. Sometimes, they are not even documented at all. All this doesn't help with workflow one bit. With Logic you could be recording audio, Virtual instruments and MIDI instruments. You'll be using virtual effects plug-ins and, perhaps, external classic effects units hardware. You'll be automating volume, pan and all the parameters of your plug-ins. You'll be musician, engineer, producer, mixing and mastering engineer all in one. The sheer complexity of the software means that many useful functions are hidden from view, often deep in nested menus and obscure Key Commands.

The book is divided into chapters covering most of Logic's areas – but don't regard this as a book that's only useful when you want to look up a particular way of working. Dip into it, keep it by the bed or read it while having breakfast. You'll stumble across new ways of working and Key Commands that you didn't know existed. While writing the book the author was heard to exclaim on more than one occasion 'Well – I never knew that!' Many of the tips apply to several different areas of Logic, whereas others are specific to one window or editor. All are useful to the Logic user.

Over many years of use, the author has searched out useful tips and trick to help get the most from Logic. This book is the result of many hours of puzzled frowns, bitten nails and years of research. Read the book from cover to cover or dip into individual sections – whichever way you use the book, it will improve your workflow and increase your productivity, and pleasure, when using this powerful and fascinating piece of software.

Acknowledgements

I'd like to thank the following for their invaluable help in preparing this book. The on-line Logic community, Christine Wilhelmy at Apple, Mike Senior, Andy Jones and last, but not least, Sara Rönneke for the support, help and advice without which I'd still be scratching my head and shouting, to no-one in particular, 'why doesn't that work the way it should?'

This book is dedicated to my parents William and Mary.

Contents

Setting up, optimization and templates

The first problem new users to Logic have to solve is usually one of set-up. Getting audio into and out of the program can, at first, cause much head scratching. Then after the Audio comes the MIDI and the puzzle begins once more. This chapter contains tips and tricks that can get you up and running with Logic as soon as you have everything connected and powered on. It may seem obvious, but before you try any of the tips in this chapter check that you have connected all the leads correctly and powered on all your equipment. If I had a Euro for every time I've solved a problem by switching on an Interface or plugging in a USB lead I wouldn't need to write this book! It also pays to read the, usually short, manuals that come with any third-party Audio or MIDI interfaces to make sure everything is set-up OK.

Drivers

CoreAudio and CoreMIDI, Apple's Operating System (OS) level software is the 'glue' that binds together Logic and any third-party Audio or MIDI gear you have. The third-party company writes a software CoreAudio or CoreMIDI driver that communicates with the Macintosh's OS. All Logic has to do is to communicate with these drivers to use the Audio and MIDI hardware. It's important that you use the correct drivers; otherwise you may have problems straight away.

Which OS?

Although some users are still using Mac OS9 or earlier, these days the majority will be using a variant of OSX. Which version you use depends on your Mac – though versions 10.2 ('Jaguar') onwards provide the CoreAudio and CoreMIDI protocols essential for working with Logic. Occasionally, a version of Logic will force an upgrade of OS; though many users prefer to leave the upgrades until absolutely necessary. This 'if it 'ain't broke, don't fix it' approach has some merits – you'll nearly always have fewer problems when you are not at the cutting edge of technological advance. Also be aware that any third-party plug-ins will also usually need upgrading when you change the OS. If in doubt, keep an eye on the manufacturer's website.

Use the correct driver for the correct version of the OS and Logic

Once you've installed the drivers, you should visit the hardware vendor's website right away and download the latest and/or correct versions of the driver. Each version of Logic and/or the OS can need different driver versions.

Check that the drivers are loaded correctly

OSX has a program, Audio MIDI setup, which is where you'll see the CoreAudio and
CoreMIDI drivers you have installed on your Mac. If you run this program and check
everything is OK, Logic will be able to find the correct drivers when it loads. This will
avoid a lot of grief later on. You'll find this program in the Applications/Utilities menu.

Figure 1.1

Audio

You may want to set the System output to 'Built-in audio'. This will make sure that
Operating syetem warnings will not be played through your audio interface.

MIDI

If you connect your audio interface and plug in all your MIDI gear you can use the
Rescan MIDI button to get all of your equipment displayed in the MIDI devices window (Figure 1.2).

    You can see your MIDI interfaces and the Ports the MIDI gear is connected to.
If the automatic detection doesn't succeed, you can manually add devices using the
'Add device' button. You can then rename the external device ('Yamaha DX7') and
drag the virtual cables as shown in Figure 1.3.

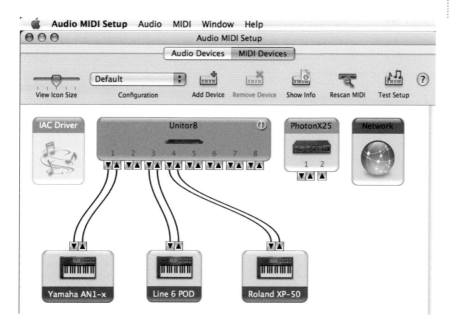

Figure 1.2

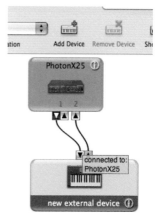

Figure 1.3

Keeping up to date

You should run Software Update (when connected to the Internet) regularly to check for Logic Updates. It's also a good idea to go to the website of your Audio, MIDI and Controller hardware manufacturers to see if there are any updates available.

The 'other' book

Logic's manuals are available from the programs Help menu (Figure 1.4). They are PDF files and can also be accessed from the Apple website; see Appendix 3.

The manuals are also installed with Logic – though they can be a little hard to find! If you find the Logic application in the Applications folder and hold down the Control key and click on the Logic application (or right-click on it), you'll see a menu (Figure 1.5).

Figure 1.4

Figure 1.5

Select 'Show package Contents'. A window opens. If you navigate the folder structure, you'll find a nested folder called 'resources'. Inside this folder, you'll find the Logic manuals in PDF format.

Figure 1.6

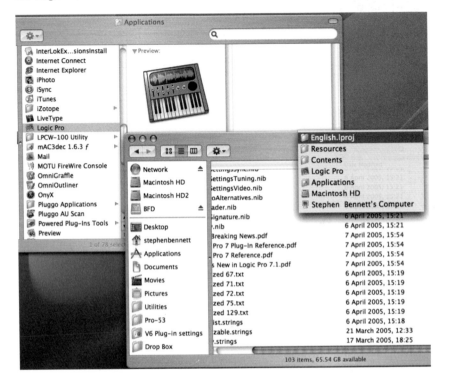

Operating system optimization

Apple's OSX is a version of the UNIX operating system. There are a few maintenance tasks that you should perform on a regular basis. If you do these, you're less likely to have software or disk access problems – both are important when using Logic.

Repairing permissions

As OSX is a relatively secure OS and you can have several different users. OSX keeps track of who can have access to files by setting permissions on files and disks. These can get corrupted and cause various problems. You may have problems installing software or strange disk-based errors may occur – such as Logic not being able to access audio files. You should repair permissions often – at least once a week. Here's how you do it.

Run the Disk Utility program from the /Applications/Utilities folder

- Select a disk
- Click on 'Repair disk'
- You'll see a progress bar appear and any permissions problems will be fixed.

Figure 1.7

Maintenance scripts

In daily use, OSX stores a lot of information in temporary files. If you leave your Mac on all the time, small shell scripts, called 'maintenance tasks', run automatically daily, weekly and monthly to delete these logs and other temporary files. You can regain a lot of disk space running these scripts if you haven't done them for a long time. Here's how you do it.

Figure 1.8

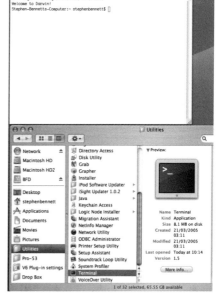

Run the Terminal from the /Applications/Utilities folder.

The daily script
- Type 'sudo sh /etc/daily' (without the quotes)
- Enter your administrator password.
- The script will run.

The weekly script
- Type 'sudo sh /etc/weekly' (without the quotes)
- Enter your administrator password.
- The script will run. – it will take longer than the daily script.

The monthly script
- Type 'sudo sh /etc/monthly' (without the quotes)
- Enter your administrator password.
- The script will run. – it will take longer than the monthly script.

The Logic Setup Assistant

Logic's Setup Assistant is a simple way to create Logic Songs (to be used as an Autoload or a Song Template (see Chapter 3). It uses the information stored in the Audio MIDI setup program detailed earlier in the chapter to create Logic Songs based around your actual set-up.

Using the Logic Setup Assistant

Run the Logic Setup Assistant from the menu item Logic Pro>Preferences>Start Logic Setup Assistant. A window will appear asking you if you wish to run the program. Click on 'Start Assistant'. Logic will close and the assistant will load. Follow through the questions and click on 'Next' at each window to continue. The assistant will run you through the various stages detailed below.

Figure 1.9

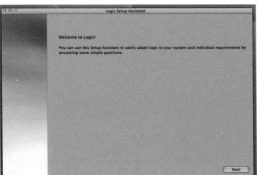

Detect devices

The assistant will ask if you have your MIDI and Audio interfaces are connected. Click on 'Yes'.

Audio

This will ask you which Audio devices you have installed that you wish to use. You could create a Song with any or all of your installed interfaces.

Core Audio Mixer Setup

In this window you can choose how many Audio Tracks, Busses and other Logic objects you wish you have in a song. The number of inputs and outputs here depends on how many physical ins and outs you have on your Audio interface.

Figure 1.10

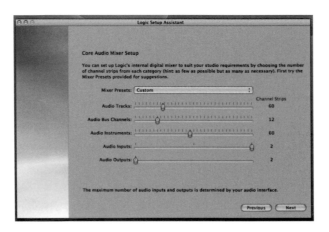

Audio Inputs

How many you can use also depends on your Audio interface. Logic helpfully suggests some set-ups you may want to use here.

Key commands

If you have used Logic before select 'Do not change existing Key commands'. Otherwise, select a suitable option. You can also import Key commands from another preference file here.

Screensets

You will want to adjust these to your personal preference later, so just click 'Next' here.

MIDI devices

If you have powered up and connected your MIDI devices (synthesizers, effects etc) and installed them correctly, they will show up here.

When the summary window appears, click on Finish. Logic will re-load.

Now go to the 'File' menu, choose 'Save as Template', and save this song as a Template (see later in the Chapter). If you call it 'Autoload', this is the Song that Logic will load when it first boots.

Aggregate devices

Logic (under OSX 10.4 or later) can create Aggregate devices. These are a group of two or more Audio and/or MIDI interfaces that appear to Logic as though they were one combined device.

Aggregate devices are created in the Audio MIDI setup program detailed earlier in the chapter. Open the program and run the Audio>Aggregate devices editor.

Figure 1.11

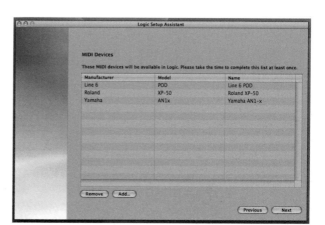

Figure 1.12

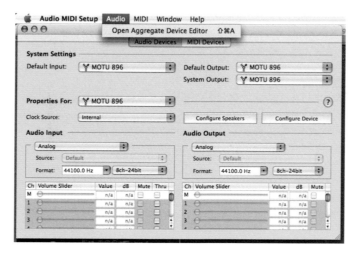

You'll see a list of all connected and installed devices. Select the ones you wish to use. Rename the device (Figure 1.13).

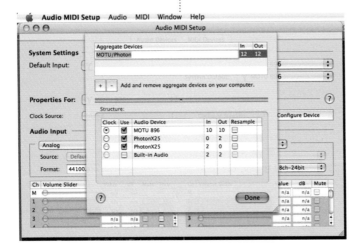

Figure 1.13

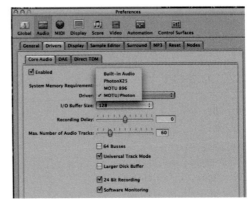

Figure 1.14

You'll see that this new aggregate device ('MOTU/Photon') has 12 inputs and outputs – The MOTU has 10, the Alesis Photon 2. Close the editor window. You can now choose this device in Logic's Audio menu>Audio hardware and drivers window.

Speeding up Logic
Depending on the power of your computer and its Video card, you may want to try these tips to improve the performance of your system.

Switch off 'Anti-aliased text' in the Preferences>Display window
This will speed up screen redraws. It's especially useful on pre-G5 Macintoshes.

Turn off Airport, and Bluetooth
They both use processing power better directed towards plug-ins.

Close all unnecessary programs and Widgets
Logic uses a lot of memory and programs running in the background eat up precious RAM.

Disable all anti Virus software
This type of software is constantly checking the hard drive, thus reducing the amount of bandwidth available for recording.

AU (Audio Unit) validation
When you first run Logic, it checks that any third party AU plug-ins pass the stringent AU validation criteria set out by Apple. If they all pass, Logic will boot normally. However, if they fail, Logic will disable the AU plug-ins. If this happens, you should check with the plug-in company whether there is a 'Logic 7 or later' version.

You can, however, allow failed plug-ins to be used in Logic. Be aware though that you do this at your own risk; unstable plug-ins can cause Logic to crash.

Enabling plug-ins that have failed the AU validation Start the Logic AU Manager from the Logic Pro>Start Logic AU Manager menu item. Logic will quit and the AU manager loads.

Enable failed AU plug-ins by clicking on the Use check box
When you have enabled all the plug-ins you want, click on OK. Logic will reload and the new AU plug-ins will be available in the usual way.

Other hardware

Hard drives

It's useful to have a second fast (7200rpm or greater) hard drive to store all your audio and Logic Song files on. Not only does this make backing up easier, but also it separates the throughput of data to disk from the OS and EXS24 sample loading. This extra drive could be internal to the Mac or it could be an external Firewire (400 or 800) or USB 2.x drive. USB 1.x is too slow for Audio recording.

Which Audio interface?

Although there are a lot of different kinds of audio interface on the market, these can be broken down into a few groupings which should help you decide which is right for your needs. The main issues are Number of Inputs, number of outputs, USB, Firewire or PCI.

Number of inputs

The more inputs you have, the more audio signals you can feel into Logic.
- You only need 2 inputs if you only want to record a mono or stereo signal.
- You'll need more inputs if you want to record a whole band, drums or return the signal from several hardware effects units, such as Reverbs and Compressors, back into Logic.
- You'll need more outputs if you want to produce a surround sound output (5:1 needs 6 outputs), you need to send signals to several hardware effects units or need to set up complex monitor mixes for band members (8 outputs can produce 8 different monitor mixes if you use a separate send per output.)

Firewire or USB 2.0 connection.

The high-speed interfaces are useful if you need portability. They can often be powered from the computer so you don't need a separate power supply unit. This is especially useful for Laptop users. These usually are equipped with 2-8 analog outputs plus they often have 2-8 digital outputs.

PCI Interfaces

These fit on an internal card in the Mac – so they are not suitable for Laptops or any other Macs without PCI cards. They often can support many more outputs and inputs – 24 is not uncommon.

Using the Mac's internal sound

You can choose to use the Mac's internal sound card. You select it in the Audio hardware and drivers window (from the main Audio menu)

The quality of the inputs on the Mac are not as good as a third-party interface (and not all Macs have them anyway) , but the output is adequate for monitoring, If you are bouncing down mixes to disk in Logic, you won't need any extra outputs. You can also use the digital interface on some Macs to send a signal to a digital to

Tip

Use a large capacity external drive to clone your audio drive and system drive as a safety backup. Use a program like carbon Copy Cloner for this.

Tip

You may also need separate drives for large disk-streamed 'Rompler' plug-ins. It's not unusual for each library to need its own dedicated disk.

Tip

You can often increase the number of ins and outs by using an 8-channel analog to digital expander box and plug it into the ADAT socket of the interface. These extra ins and outs appear in Logic as one combined set.

Info

Interfaces often have monitor sections, latency free monitors, headphone outputs and DSP plug-ins onboard that can be used in Logic.

Figure 1.15

analog converter. You'll also find that you can't get the lowest buffer size using the internal sound facilities.

Templates

Logic can store user-defined songs as 'Templates'. You may, for example, have a template that you use for multi-track recording, one for stereo recording, one for general use, one for mastering and so on. Templates are just normal Logic songs, like the Autoload Song, that are stored in a specific location and can be recalled at will.

Info

Logic's Templates are stored in the Users/Library/Application Support/Logic/Song Templates.

Tip

You can create sub-folders in the Users/Library/Application Support/Song Template folder to keep similar Templates grouped together.

Tip

Use Logic's Set-up assistant to create different Templates.

Saving Templates

Create a Logic Song you want to use as a Template. In the example below, the Template has been set-up for recording 16 audio inputs. Each Logic song can have it's own Screensets and MIDI and Audio set-up. You can easily create different Logic Songs for use as Templates using Logic's Setup Assistant – see Chapter 1 for more details. Once the song has been created and modified to your satisfaction, save it from the File>Save as Template menu item.

Figure 1.16

Loading Templates

Select the File>New menu item. Make sure that the 'Use song template' parameter is ticked. You can now select a Template from the 'Template' pull-down menu.

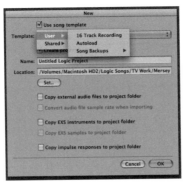

Figure 1.17

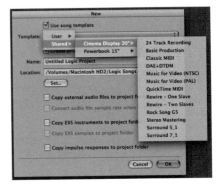

Figure 1.18

Projects and back-ups

Although Logic stores any recordings as a Song, which is a single file, most Logic Songs will usually have many other files associated with them. If you just save a Song using the File>Save menu item, audio files will be saved in the directory defined by the Audio>Set Audio Record Path window. Other associated files could reside in other locations.

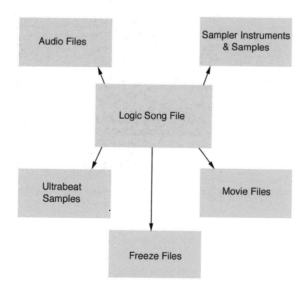

Figure 2.1
Files associated with a Logic song

It's better to save a Logic session as a Project. A Project is a collection of Logic Song and all associated files collected together into a single folder and sub-folders. Apart from the usefulness of collecting all of Logic's files together in one place when backing-up, it's also useful to do this when you want to send a Logic song to collaborators. 'Save as Project' is found in the File manu (Figure 2.2).

Figure 2.2

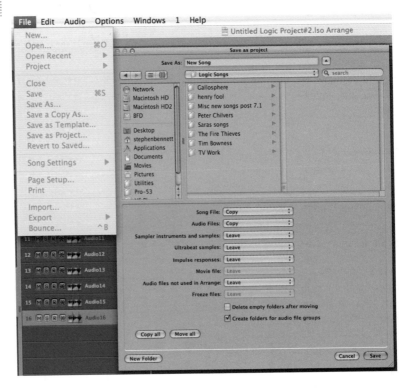

As you can see, you can choose which associated files to save (or collect) into a Logic Project folder. Which you choose depends on what you want to do with the Song.

If you want to work with this song only on the Macintosh it was recorded on or another Macintosh running the same version of Logic and has the same samples
In this case, you'd probably only want to Copy Audio files, Freeze files and, if you are using them, any Movie files into the Project folder. Samples and Impulse responses (for Space Designer) can be left in their default folders.

If you want to work with this song on another system where you can't be sure it has the same version of Logic and associated samples
In this case, you'd want to Copy Audio files, Freeze files and, if you are using them, any Movie files into the Project folder along with samples and Impulse responses (for Space Designer).

In both the above cases you can choose to separate out audio files not being used in the Arrange page.

Project manager

The Project manager is one part of Logic that many users never explore. In it's basic form it's a database of all the Audio files, EXS instruments and samples, Plug-in settings, Movie files and Song files on all the hard drives on your Macintosh. Once these files are found, you can find, load and move theses files around. The first time you run the Project manager, you run the Functions>Scan menu item. The Project manager will then scan through all your hard drives and produce a database of all your Logic related files – the database is updated whenever you boot Logic.

One of the benefits of the Project Manager after you've scanned your disks is that Logic will find your EXS24 sampler files much more quickly and they will load much faster.

Saving backups

To make sure you don't lose an important previous version of your song, you can get Logic to save up to 100 previous versions of a Song. You set this amount in the Song handling Preferences window.

Audio file housekeeping

During a recording session, you'll accumulate lots of audio that won't be used in the final mix. All these audio files take up hard disk space. Logic has various features that can help out. Open the Audio window from the Audio menu. Most of these functions work when you've selected an audio file or Region in the Audio window.

Tip

You can use this feature to reclaim disk space by separating out unused files and then deleting them from the hard disk. You must also make sure you've deleted them from the Audio window using the Audio window Edit>Select unused menu item and press Delete to delete these pointers to the files. If you don't do this, Logic will search for these files every time you load the song.
If you group files in the Audio window into Groups (Audio window>View>Create Group) you can get Logic to sort these into sub-folders in the Project folder.

The Audio window Audio file menu
Optimize File(s) This will delete any fragments of any selected audio files not used the Arrange page.
Delete Files(s) This deletes any selected files. See the section below on the Edit window for selection criteria.

The Edit window
There are various selection criteria in this menu to help you find files not being used in a Particular Song.
Select Unused Use this function to select all files NOT being used in the Song.
Select files... This function has a sub-menu which allows you to use various criteria for selecting files. These will help you make sure you don't delete files used in other Songs.

Tip

You can see any selected Regions that contain audio files actual location in the Finder using the Arrange
Page > Audio > Show selected audio files in Finder.

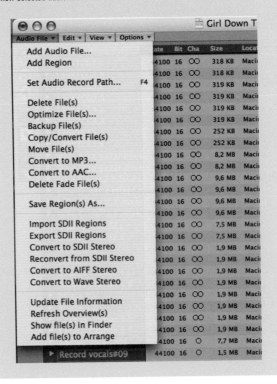

Getting around in Logic

There are many ways to perform tasks in Logic, which can, at first, seem daunting. However, as this is part of the highly cusomisable personality of Logic, it means you can usually work in any way you want. If a particular way of working offends, then change it! This chapter covers tips on getting around Logic's functions and should help you to improve workflow.

Toolbox

You can hide and show the Toolbox using the Arrange page View menu.

You can set up two assignable Tools per Screenset by Apple-key-clicking on the Tool you require. Then when you press the Apple key, the mouse cursor will change to the pre-selected tool.

If you have a mouse with a right mouse button you can assign it to open the Toolbox at the cursor position from the Preferences>Global>Open Toolbox menu item

If you set the Preferences>Global parameter to 'Is assignable to a tool' and you have a mouse with a right mouse button, you can store three assignable tools per Screenset. The first is the tool you select by left clicking on the Toolbox. The second you set up by Apple-clicking on the Tool you require. Clicking on the required tool on the Toolbox with the right mouse key chooses the third.

Scrolling with the Mouse

The scroll wheel can be used for scrolling up and down in a window. Holding down the Alt key while you do this zooms the tracks vertically, whilst holding down the Apple key scrolls along the Song's timeline. Holding down the Shift and Alt keys while scrolling, zooms the window horizontally.

If you hold down the Control and Shift key in a Window, the cursor becomes a 4-pointed arrow. You can now scroll around the window in both horizontal and vertical directions.

Link

To make sure all open windows are showing the same data, you need to make sure the Link icon is 'ON' for all windows.

Figure 3.1

Logic's link feature can seem a little complicated – there are basically two modes of operation.

Link mode

If you click once on the Link Icon, the window always displays the same contents as the top window, if that is possible. Here's an example of what this means.

If you have a Matrix editor, an Event editor and an Arrange page open, and the Link icon is, clicking on a region on the Arrange page will show the following Event editor window. Note that the Event editor shows the same 'level' of data as the Arrange page.

Figure 3.2

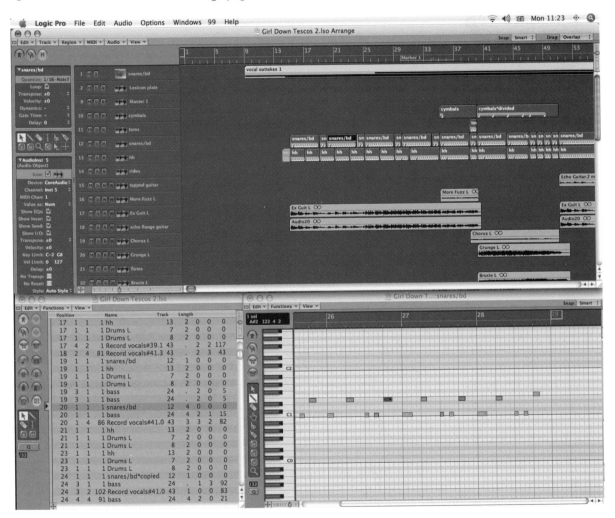

Now click on a note in the Matrix editor. You will see the Event list editor will change to show the same notes as the Matrix editor, i.e. it is at the same 'level' of data.

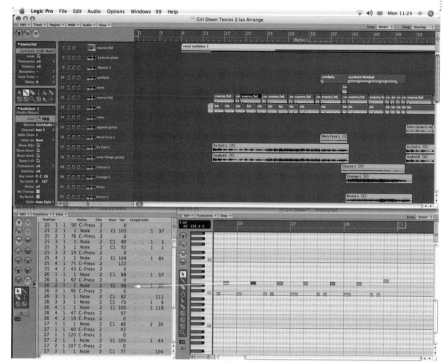

Figure 3.3

Link - Show Contents mode

If you double click on the Link icon the behavior of the windows changes. If you have the same Matrix editor, Event editor and Arrange page open and the Link icon is yellow, clicking on the Arrange page will show the following Event editor window.

Note that the Event editor shows data one 'level' below that of the Arrange page, i.e. the note data of the selected region in the Arrange page. Now click on a note in the Matrix editor. You will see the Event list editor will keep the same data as the Matrix editor. You cannot have one 'level' below that of MIDI events!

Figure 3.4

If you switch on both the Running man and the Link icon in 'Link-Show Contents mode' you can force the editors to display the notes of each region currently being played on a selected track as the song position line passes over it.

Linking and the Environment

If you click once on the Link icon in the Environment, selecting an instrument in the Arrange window will select that instrument object in the Environment even if it has to change layers to do it. This is useful if you select a modifier, such as an arpeggiator in the Arrange page, and you want to modify its parameters from the Environments Parameter box. You can have many windows open with different Link Settings saved as a Screenset.

Figure 3.5

Running man - making sure all your open windows are synchronized

To make sure all the open windows are showing the same section of the Song, make sure the Running man icon is 'ON'

Setting a default editor

Depending on the way you work, you may want the Matrix (Piano Roll), List edit or Score editor to open when you double click on a Region. You set this behaviour in the Global Preferences Editing window.

Easy dragging

It's easy to accidentally drag Regions or notes vertically instead of horizontally or vice versa in the Arrange, Matrix and Score editors. To stop this happening, you can limit scrolling to one direction only from the Global>Editing preferences window.

Playing music from the computer keyboard

If you don't have a MIDI or other controller music keyboard handy, you can use the computer keyboard. You can set the Caps Lock Key to show the on-screen keyboard from the Global Preferences Caps Lock Key window.

Key commands

Key Commands are one of Logic's most important features – however, because some of them are often poorly documented they are not always used to the full. It's important to realise that some functions in Logic are *only* available via Key Commands. Open the Key Commands window from the Logic Pro>Preferences menu.

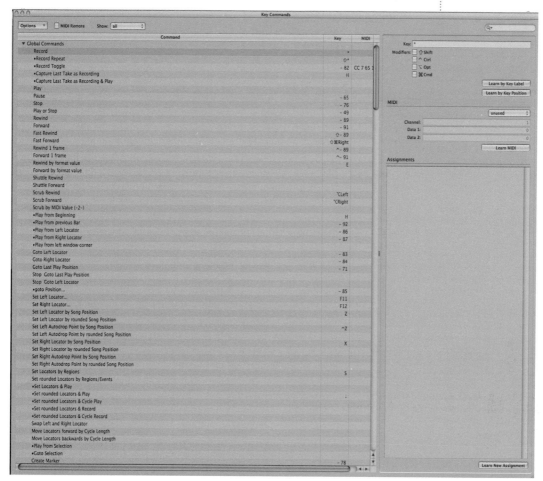

Figure 3.6 (above)
Key commands window

Logic functions which are only available as Key Commands

These have a 'dot' next to them in the Key Commands window (Figure 3.7).

Figure 3.7

Finding what Key Command is assigned to which computer key

Make sure 'Learn by Key label' and 'Learn by Key Position' are not selected (Figure 3.8). When you press a key on the computer keyboard, the Key Command it's been assigned to will be highlighted.

Assigning Key Commands to the numeric keypad

Click on the 'Learn by key position' button and select the Key Command you wish to assign. You'll see that the ASCII code for the key is displayed.

Figure 3.8

Figure 3.9

Key Commands template

You can copy all your Key Commands into a text editor and print them out. Use the Key Commands Option Pull down menu, Copy key Commands to Clipboard item.

Importing Key Commands

From the same menu, you can import Key Commands from any Logic preferences file. Using this feature you can carry your own personal Key Commands around with you.

Undo and Redo

Most procedures in Logic can be Undone. The number of Edit>Undo steps is defined In the Global preferences window. Note that the greater the number of Undo steps you define the greater the memory used to store these steps. The Edit>UNDO history window allows you to undo edits back to a specific point and redo them again if you're not happy with the results. Not all of Logic's functions can be undone; though Logic will usually warn you if this is so.

Markers

Markers are very useful for defining various sections of a Song. You can place a Marker at the Choruses, Verses, Bridges and so on. Markers can also contain text information – each Marker has a little word processor, where you can type in helpful information. You may want to remember how a guitar was recorded, how a vocal take was done, what settings you used on a non programmable hardware box and so on.

Markers are most easily created and manipulated from the Arrange page>Global Tracks menu item. You can choose which Global Tracks are displayed from the Global

Figure 3.10

Track Components menu – make sure the 'Marker' parameter is checked (Figure 3.10).

Markers can be created by highlighting a Region and clicking on the 'From Regions' button or from the Options> Marker menu items (Figure 3.11).

You can edit them by opening the marker list from the Option>Markers menu item (Figure 3.12).

Figure 3.11

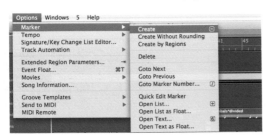

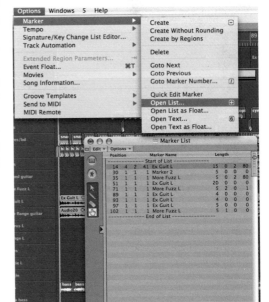

Figure 3.12

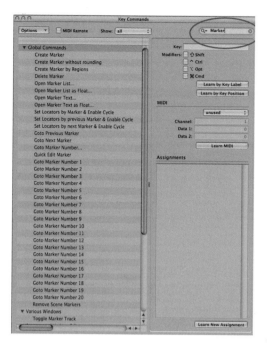

Figure 3.13

Tip

Use the set of marker Key Commands to create, move around to and open the Marker List. See figure left.

Figure 3.14

Here you can edit the start point of each Marker directly by double clicking on the Position field. You can define how the Position is displayed from the Options menu. You may want it in Bars or SMPTE units (Figures 3.13 and 3.14).

Figure 3.15

Double clicking on a Marker opens a text editor window (Figure 3.15).

Here you can edit the Marker text. As you can see the Marker window is a small text editor. You can change the font,

Figure 3.16

text size. The Face menu (Figure 3.16) allows you to change various Text parameters and the text colours.

If the Running man icon is highlighted and the Marker window is open, the text in the Marker window will change as the Song progresses (and the Markers change).

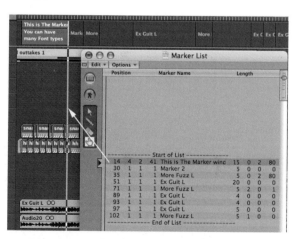

Figure 3.17

- Use the Key Commands 'Set Locators By Previous Marker' and 'Set Locators By Next Marker' and 'Enable Cycle' to quickly move through a Song. If Logic is playing when you use these Key Commands, the SPL will move to the new Marker and cycle round the Locators.
- Drag a marker down towards the Arrange page region area to delete it.
- Drag the cycle region to the Marker area to create a Marker the length of the cycle region.

Figure 3.18

Audio window groups

In a complex song, you may have hundreds of audio files in the Audio window. This can make tracking down individually files a nightmare. Fortunately, you can sort audio files into groups, just like folders in OSX. To group files highlight the files you want (Figure 3.19). Then use the menu item View>Create Group. You'll be asked to name the group (Figures 3.20 and 3,21).

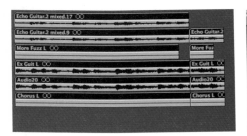
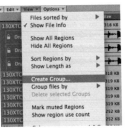

Left to right: Figures 3.19, 3.20 and 3.21

You can see the files within the group by clicking on the triangle to the left of the Group name.

Tip

You can also Group files using various criteria – these are chosen from the View>Group files by menu item.

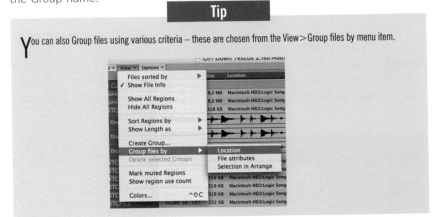

Info

Double clicking on the space under the last Track on the Arrange page will create a new Track.

Creating Tracks and Objects

You can create Tracks and Objects in the Arrange page from the Track>Create Multiple Tracks menu. A window opens. You can create as many tracks as you want of whatever type in mono or stereo. These are placed in the Arrange page and the Environment.

Figure 3.23

Figure 3.24

Figure 3.25

Snapping and Dragging

When moving Regions around the Arrange page or notes in the Matrix editor how they butt up against each other is determined by the settings of the Snap and Drag pull down menus at the top right of the respective pages (Figures 3.24 and 3.25).

The Snap menu

Using this menu you can determine the behaviour of the drag.

- Smart – this will usually allow you to drag a region to where you want it to be. You can always make the movement finer using the modifier keys described above.
- Bar – this limits the dragging to individual bars.
- Beat – this limits the dragging to individual beats.
- Format – if you have the View>SMPTE Time ruler switched on, you can drag and snap to using the SMPTE values.
- You can also snap to ticks, frames and quarter frames (QF).

Drag menu

This defines how regions butt up to regions they are dragged against (Figure 3.26).

- *Overlap*

  This mode preserves the region size when dragged – even if overlapping another region (Figures 3.27 and 3.28).

- *No Overlap*

  If you drag a region over another region using this mode, the second region is truncated in size (Figures 3.29 and 3.30).

- *X-fade*

  This mode automatically cross-fades two adjacent regions. It's useful if you want to remove clicks from the transition. You can also use the crossfade tool for more complex fades.

- *Shuffle L and Shuffle R*

  These two modes will automatically butt up a dragged region to the left and right respectively of another region automatically.

Moving, copying, cutting, deleting and resizing regions

Moving, copying and resizing are all done on an invisible grid set by the bar and beat settings in the Transport bar (left). You can change how fine this grid is holding down the following modifier keys while performing the required function.

Ctrl   Moves in ticks
Ctrl+shift   No Grid. Movement is unrestrained

Nudging Regions and notes

There's a whole series of nudge event Key Commands for moving Regions and note events very precisely (Figure 3.31). They allow you to choose the type of the nudge – for example, SMPTE time and beat, bar and Tick.

Figure 3.26

Figure 3.27

Figure 3.28

Figure 3.29

Figure 3.30

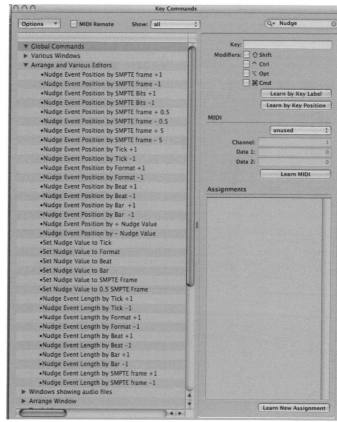

Figure 3.31

Screensets

These are one of Logic's most famous features and are essential for making the most of the multi-window approach of the program. They are also useful if you have a small screen. Screensets are stored with a Song and you can copy Screensets between Songs using the Environment menu's Options>Import settings menu item. This opens a window where you can choose what to import and the Song that you wish to import from.

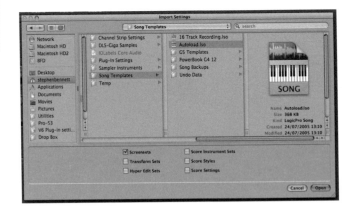

Figure 3.32

Screensets can be copied and pasted from the Windows>Screenset>Copy Screenset menu. Then choose a new Screenset and Paste it there from the same menu.

Useful Key Commands for Screensets

- Next/Previous Key Command – sometimes it's quicker to move around the different Screensets using this Key Command.
- You can Lock, Copy and Paste Screensets using the respective Key Commands.
- Revert to Current Screenset – if you have moved things around in an unlocked Screenset, this Key Command brings the Screenset back to the way it was when you first selected it.

Selecting things

Most of Logic's windows have several options for selecting items in their Edit menus (Figure 3.33). These make it easy to select, for example, muted objects or all Regions after the SPL. Most of these select options have corresponding Key Commands.

Lining up windows

While you can drag windows around using the normal Macintosh methods, Logic has several pre-set window arrangements. You can select these from the Windows menu or use the corresponding Key Commands.

Figure 3.33

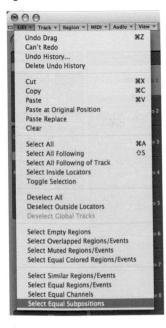

Figure 3.34

Tip

You can then use the Crop Regions outside Marquee Selection Key Command to split the Region.

The Marquee tool

This tool (Figure 3.35) is especially useful for selecting parts of Regions. If you choose the tool and draw the tool in a rectangle across a Region, it will be selected (Figure 3.36).

Figure 3.35

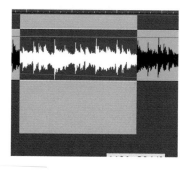

Figure 3.36

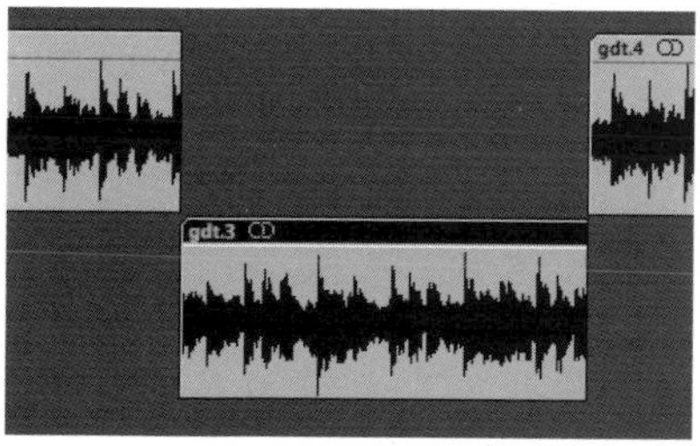

Figure 3.37

Once selected, you can use the Arrow tool to drag the selected Region, hold down the Option Key and copy it, Mute it or perform any of the regular Region editing commands (Figure 3.37).

Selecting windows without bringing them to the front

You can select objects in any background window without bringing that window to the front. You need to click and hold the mouse to stop the window becoming the focus (Figure 3.38).

Figure 3.38

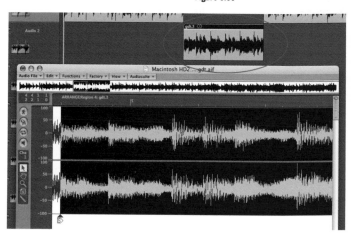

Figure 3.39

Copying between songs

Logic can open many songs at the same time and Regions can be freely copied between each Song. To do this, Load each Song into Logic.

Arrange the screen layout so that an Arrange page for each Song are visible seen and the Tracks you wish to copy Regions to are visible. Drag the Regions from the source Song to the Destination Song.

Figure 3.40

The Finder Dock and what to do with it

OSX's Dock feature in the Finder is very useful for launching applications. But it can get in the way if you are using a program like Logic that requires a lot of screen real estate. There are several ways to improve the situation. These changes are made in the Dock section of the System preferences application.

Figure 3.41

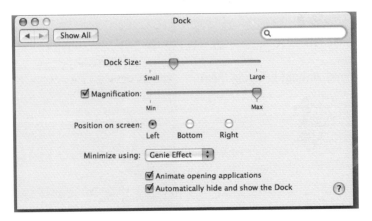

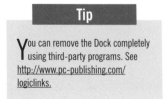

Tip

You can remove the Dock completely using third-party programs. See http://www.pc-publishing.com/logiclinks.

- The Dock defaults to appear at the bottom of the screen. This can get in the way of using the window sliders. You may want to move it to the left or right side using the Position button.
- Automatically hide and show the dock. Using this option makes the Dock disappear until you pass the mouse over it. Using the Magnification slider allows you to have a small dock – unless you move the mouse over a specific icon. Use the Dock Size slider to resize the dock.

Figure 3.42

Play and Record Key Commands

While you can use the mouse to perform most record and play functions, you can speed up workflow by using some of the useful Key Commands relating to these functions.

Play

If you use any of the Key Commands for Play, you can use a Bluetooth keyboard (or one with a long lead) to Control Logic remotely. This is particularly useful if you are recording with a microphone and need to get as far away from the computer and monitor as possible. As you can see from the dot at the left of the list of Key Commands, many of these are only available as Key Commands.

Figure 3.43 (left)

Figure 3.44

Record

The same advantages apply here as for the Play Key Commands options. The computer keyboard can double as a remote record controller using these Key Commands.

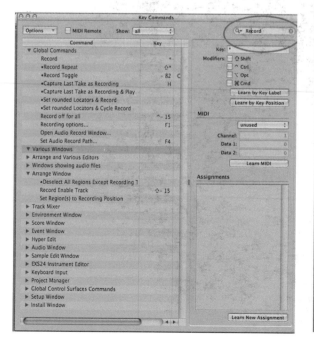

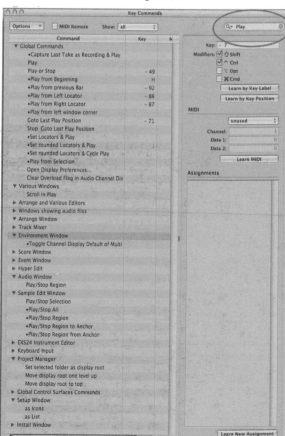

Selection/Deselection Key Commands

All windows have various Key Commands that help with selection of Regions, notes or other objects.

Figure 3.45

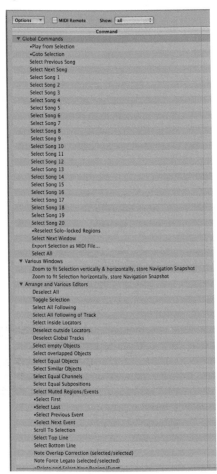

Figure 3.46

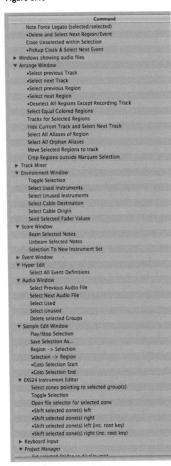

Figure 3.47

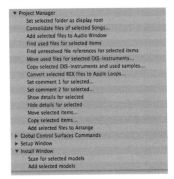

Figure 3.48

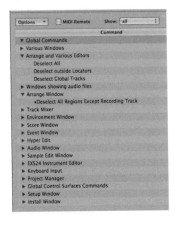

Many of these only exist as key Commands and are quite specialized. They are particularly useful if you are performing repetitive tasks.

Parameter boxes

When you select a Region, Track, object or event in one of Logic's windows a Parameter box will detail the various parameters you can modify relating to that object. You can usually change values by dragging the numbers up and down, double-clicking on the value and entering the value directly, or holding down on the little arrows to bring up a value selection menu.

The small triangle on the Parameter box opens or closes the box. This is useful if you are using Logic on a small screen.

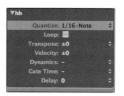   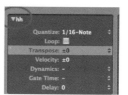

Region Parameter box

(left to right) Figures 3.49, 3.50, 3.51 and 3.52

This displays the Parameters available from any selected Region or Regions. These parameters will be different depending on the Region type.

Figure 3.53 (left)
MIDI Region (on an Instrument track)

Figure 3.54 (below)
Audio Region

Figure 3.55
Double-clicking on the name allows you to rename a Region or Regions

Figure 3.56

Figure 3.57

Audio Regions: The Follow tempo Parameter only appears when you select an audio Region that was recorded directly into Logic 7 or later. It allows audio files to change tempo when you change the tempo of the song, just like MIDI data (Figure 3.56).

Audio Regions: The Loop Parameter will loop a Region until it meets another Region on the same Track. You can also loop Regions using by moving the mouse to the top right of the Region and dragging (Figure 3.57).

Audio Regions: The Fade Parameter is active with audio Regions. You can choose a Fade type and value. You can also edit fades created by the Crossfade tool here (Figures 3.58 and 3.59).

Audio Regions: The Curve Parameter defines the slope of the crossfade. 0 is a linear type, increasing the value creates exponential curves (Figures 3.60 and 3.61).

Figure 3.58 (above)

Figure 3.59

Figure 3.62
There is a default setting for crossfades in the general Audio preferences menu.

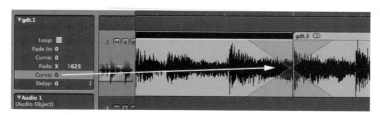

Figure 3.60 (above) and Figure 3.61(below)

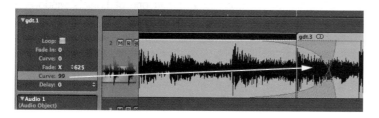

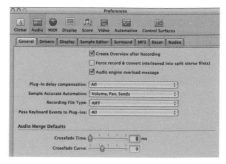

MIDI Regions: Dynamics Parameter. This Parameter can be used as a kind of MIDI version of an audio compressor.

MIDI Regions: Gate Parameter. The gate of a note refers to the time between pressing and releasing a key. The values which Logic use fall somewhere between staccato (short sharp notes) and legato (long notes). The 'Fix' value means extreme staccato, values below 100% shorten the note length, values above lengthen it. The 'Leg' value produces completely joined up playing.

MIDI Regions: Delay Parameter. This Parameter alters the time delay of selected Regions in ticks or milliseconds depending on the setting in the View menu. You can bring regions forwards or Backwards.

Info

The Instrument Track has extra Parameters – these are the same ones found on a MIDI track. As Virtual Instruments are played-back by MIDI, this makes complete sense.

Track Parameter box

The Parameters, which appear here, depend upon the type of Track selected.

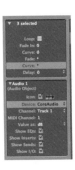

Figure 3.63
Audio Track

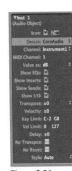

Figure 3.64
Virtual Instrument track

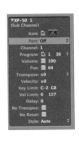

Figure 3.65
MIDI Track

Tip

Double clicking on the Instrument name opens a box where you can rename the Track.

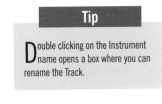

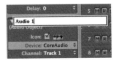

Figure 3.66
Rename the track

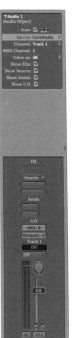

Figure 3.67 (left)
Audio file playback (including the channel strip)

Figure 3.68
Virtual Instrument playback (including the channel strip)

Tip

Audio Tracks can be of the Track, Instrument, Input,Aux,Output, Bus or Master type. The type is chosen from the Channel: parameter.

Audio Track types and Parameters

Audio Track for playback of audio files and Virtual Instruments, Inputs and Outputs

Parameters

Device You can set which Audio interface is used to play back the Audio on the Track from the Device: parameter.

Value as You can choose whether the volume displayed in dB or Numerically from the Value as: parameter.

You can show or hide various parts of the Channel Strip to make it smaller – this is very useful for smaller screens.

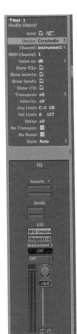

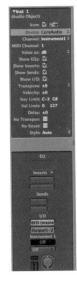

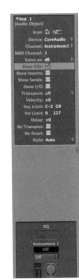

Figure 3.69a
Show or hide parts of the channel strip

MIDI Track for the playback of external MIDI hardware devices

Double clicking on the Track name opens a box where you can rename the Track (Figure 3.70). Clicking to the right of this brings up a box containing the patch names of your MIDI device if you have entered these into a Multi-Instrument.

The small triangle on the Parameter box opens or closes the box. This is useful if you are using Logic on a small screen.

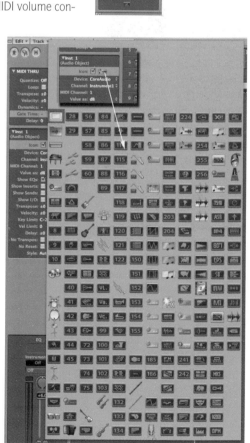

Figure 3.70

Icon Clicking, and holding, on the icon itself opens a list where you can change the icon assigned to the instrument. Holding Shift as you do this leaves the menu open when you let go of the mouse key, so you can use the cursor keys to choose the icon.

Channel This shows the MIDI channel of the selected instrument. It can be changed here with the mouse or by double clicking on the value.

Program An X in the box will transmit any changes made here to the MIDI device. The number on the right is the program change number. If you hold and click on this number, a pop up list appears from which you can select the program number. If you have assigned patch names to a Multi Instrument their names will appear here. Clicking to the left of this number will allow you to send bank select messages. You'll need to check your MIDI device handbook to see if your MIDI device uses bank select messages.

Volume An X in the box will transmit any changes to the MIDI device. MIDI volume controller data will be sent out if you change the number in the right hand column.

Pan This works in a similar way to the Vol parameter above.

Transpose You can transpose all regions on a Track using this parameter.

Velocity You can adjust the overall response to Velocity for all Regions on a track.

Key Limiter You can limit the range of notes played back by an instrument by setting a lower (left value) and higher (right value) note value here. All notes outside this range will not be played by the MIDI instrument.

Velocity limiter You can limit the volume range of any instrument by setting a lower (left value) and higher (right value) value here. All notes whose velocity lies outside this range will not be played by the instrument.

No Transpose If this is checked all Regions played by this instrument will be protected from transposition. Use this to keep drum sounds on their correct keys when transposing.

No Reset If this box is checked, no more reset messages will be sent to the instrument selected.

Style Auto Clicking on this brings up the Score styles menu which are used in the Score editor. This is normally left set to Auto.

Figure 3.71
Don't forget to give your Tracks a useful icon.
Click on the Icon and an icon list will appear.

Channel strip Presets

If you click on the little arrow to the right of 'Insert' a pull down menu appears.

Figure 3.72

These are Channel Strip presets and they are a series of saved Channel Strip configurations. Audio, Bus, Aux and Instrument Tracks will load different presets. The Virtual Instrument Channel Strips include the Instruments themselves.

Figure 3.73
This is 'Backward Bowed Piano'

Figure 3.74
You can Save your own
Channel Strip combinations

Figure 3.75
Or Copy them and paste them
into a New Channel Strip

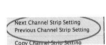

Figure 3.76
Step backwards and forwards
through Channel Strip presets
using the menu items ...

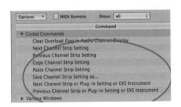

Figure 3.77
... or the Key Commands.

Recording

Audio recording

Latency tips

Recording in Logic is affected by latency, that is, the time it takes for the audio to pass through the program, plug-ins and the audio input and output. If you are recording a vocalist, for example, what they hear when monitoring in the head-phones after passing through Logic can be delayed causing a slight echo effect that can be disconcerting for the singer. If you play Virtual Instruments, you may find that there is a delay between playing a note on a keyboard and the note actually sounding. There are a couple of ways to alleviate this problem.

Reduce the I/O buffer size in the Audio preferences window

The lower the buffer size the lower the latency and thus the lower the delay to the vocalist will be. However, lowering the buffer size puts a greater strain on the CPU and will lower the number of plug-ins you can run. Go too low and you may also get CPU overloads.

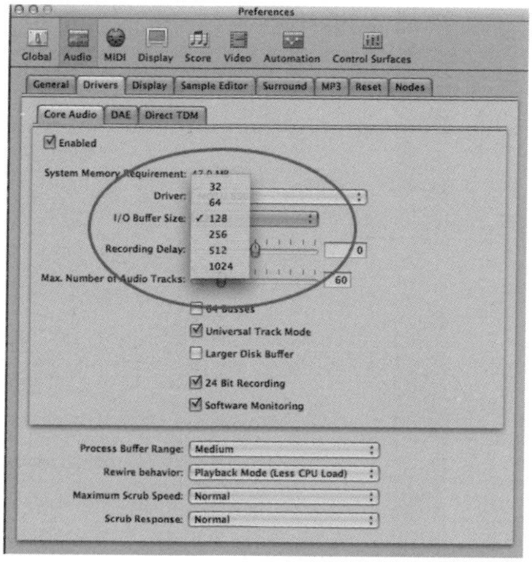

De-select Software Monitoring

When this is 'ON', audio passes through Logic and any plug-ins inserted on the recording Track. You may have set up a plug-in reverb on this Track to help out a singer, for example. All this adds to the latency and the delay effects discussed above. Turning Software Monitoring to OFF will alleviate this problem – though you can't use any plug-ins on the recording Track.

Tip

You can work out the latency in Milliseconds (ms) by the following equation.
Latency (ms) = Buffer size (samples)/Recording sample frequency.
So, for example, a buffer size of 256 and recording at 44.1kHz will give a latency of 5.8ms.
Vocals and drums will need to be recorded with latencies around 6ms. (256 buffer size).
Guitarists can usually cope with latencies up to 12ms. They are used to the delay between amplifier or sound hole and ear. (512 buffer size).
Keyboards and Virtual instruments can often be played using latencies up to 20ms (1024 buffer size).

Figure 4.1

Tip

If you want to use Software Monitoring, use a low CPU plug-in, such as the PlatinumVerb or Silververb to minimize latency.

Tip

Use an external mixer and reverb unit if you can't get the buffer settings low enough to please whoever you are recording. See below for more details.

33

CPU (Central Processing Unit) overload problems

If you are finding that you're getting CoreAudio overload messages or that the CPU monitor (Audio>System performance) monitor is hitting the red, there are a couple of things you can do to help the problem.

Freeze tracks

Freezing in Logic automatically mixes down the audio or Virtual Instrument data on a track to an audio file along with all plug-in effects. This 'combined' track is then automatically placed on the frozen Track. You can unfreeze a track at any time. Once frozen, the Track uses almost no CPU power – but you cannot edit any of the plug-ins on the Track unless you unfreeze it. You can, however edit volume and pan data. Freezing releases any CPU power used by any plug-ins on a track.

Figure 4.2

Tip

Make sure you can see the Freeze buttons on the Arrange page. They are displayed from the Arrange page View menu.

Increase buffer size

Increasing the buffer size to 512 or 1024 will relieve the load on the CPU, allowing you to use more plug-ins and Virtual instruments.

Tip

You'll probably only do this after you've finished any recording due to the latency effects as described above.

Dual processor CPU monitor/CoreAudio problems

On a dual CPU processor Mac, the Logic System performance monitor has two meters for each processor. You may occasionally find that only one processor seems to be used and as that reaches maximum, Logic may complain with CoreAudio errors. If you start Logic playing, press stop and press start again, processing will be spread evenly across both processors.

Figure 4.3   Figure 4.4

Tip

You can force Logic to use the second processor to play back a Track that uses a lot of CPU power by selecting that Track on playback.

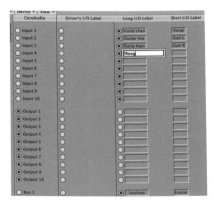

Figure 4.5

Input/Output labels

You can label your inputs, outputs and busses, so you can select these by name from an Instrument, Audio or Buss object.

Open the Audio>Audio configuration window.
Select the View>I/O labels menu item.
You can now name the inputs, outputs and busses.
And choose these in the Arrange page.

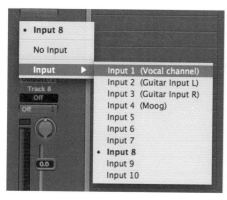

Figure 4.6

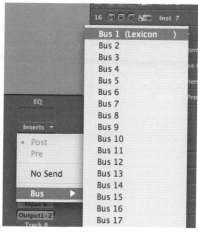

'Printing' effects onto a recording

Figure 4.7

Usually when you record, you only want to use an effect when you are monitoring, such as a reverb on vocals. Sometimes, however, you may want to record the effects along with the signal. An example of this is if you want to record a guitar through amplifier simulator directly.

Normally, you'd record into Logic using an Audio Track object. However, if you do this, any plug-ins inserted onto that object will be heard when recording, but a clean signal will be recorded. Using an Input object, however, allows the effects to be recorded along with the audio.

First select an Input object in the Arrange page.

If you don't have any Input channel objects, you can create them in the Environment. Open the Environment and create a new page – call it 'Input objects'. Create an Audio object from the New menu and double click on it to make it full size.

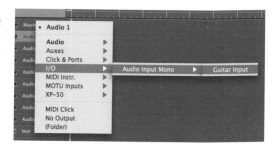

Figure 4.8

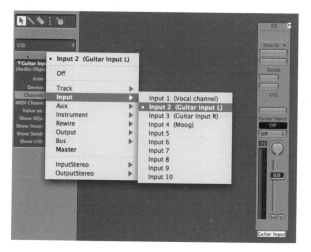

Select the object and choose an Input from the Channel pull down menu in the Parameter box. This should be the actual physical input you're guitar is plugged into. Rename the Input object to something like 'Guitar input'

Figure 4.9

Figure 4.10

Make sure the Output on the Input object is set to 'No Output'. Insert the required plug-in on this object.

Figure 4.11

In the Arrange page, select an Audio Track object.

Figure 4.12

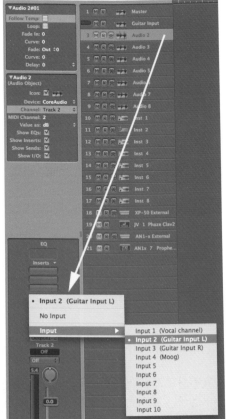

Figure 4.13

Choose the Input object as the input to the Track.

If you click on the REC button on the Audio Track object, you should hear the guitar with the plug-in on the Input object applied.

You can now record the guitar with the plug-in effects.

Figure 4.14

Tip

Make sure the buffer size (set in the Audio Preferences window) is low enough for there to be no appreciable delay when you play the guitar. You should also set Plug-in delay compensation to 'Audio tracks and Instruments' or 'Off'; otherwise Logic will try to compensate for the delay in the playback chain.

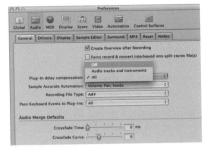

Setting the recording time

Logic deals with audio files more efficiently if you set a Maximum recording time in the Audio>Set Audio Recording Path preferences window. You can set this to the length of time you are likely to use. It can be a cause of confusion occasionally, as Logic will stop recording when it reaches this value.

Quantizing audio and beat slicing (strip silence)

You may be familiar with plug-ins and software that can take an audio file and slice it into chunks depending on various set parameters. These slices can them be moved around and quantized to create new parts. For example, you may have a 4 bar drum recording.

You may want to extract the snare and bass drum beats, move them around and change the timing. You can so this in Logic with the Strip Silence' function. First select the drum recording Region and open Strip Silence from the Arrange page Audio menu.

Figure 4.15

Figure 4.16

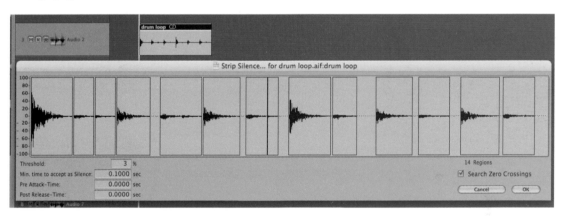

You'll see the audio sliced into individual sections. There are a few parameters that you can adjust to get the effect you desire.

The higher the Threshold the more short Regions that are produced.

You can adjust the Minimum time to accept as silence. This defines the length of a gap in the audio that is defined as silence and therefore where the cuts are made.

The Pre and Post release times can be adjusted to prevent strip silence from 'chopping' off slow attack times at the start and end of Regions created. As we are editing a drum loop, we want to keep these values as fast as possible.

Clicking on OK will generate Regions based on the settings.

If you play these Regions, you'll hear how strip silence has sliced the drum loop. If you aren't happy, select Edit>Undo and try again. You can rename the Regions to the beats they represent if you want.

Figure 4.17

Tip

If you haven't quite got each Region 'on the beat', double click on the offending Region and the Sample editor will open. Drag the' S' marker to the start of the actual audio. Close the Sample editor and the start of the audio will be exactly at the start of the Region.

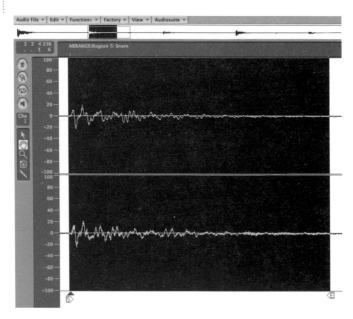

Figure 4.18

Quantizing the Regions

If you've managed to put each drum beat into it's own Region, you can then quantize the Regions. Here's how you do it. Highlight all the sliced Regions. Open the List editor – you'll see the Regions listed. If you hold down the Q button you can choose the Quantize value and quantize the Regions.

Figure 4.19

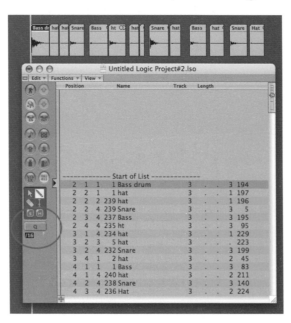

Creating and manipulating 'takes' and 'mute and cycle ' recording

A lot of Logic users work alone. It's often convenient to perform several takes of a vocal or guitar solo, choose the best bits of the take and create a 'Comp' (Compilation) of the best bits. If you are doing this alone, you may also want to loop around the recording and record each take, muting the last. Here's how you do this in Logic.

Figure 4.20

Looping around a section and recording

In the Song settings> Recording Preferences window, select 'Auto mute in cycle record' and 'Auto create in cycle record.

Set a cycle Region that you want to loop around.

Figure 4.21

Start recording and play or sing. As you reach the end of the looped Region, the SPL will move to the start of the loop again, a new recording begins and the previous recording will be muted.

When you've finished your Takes press stop. Several Tracks and muted Regions ('Takes') will be created.

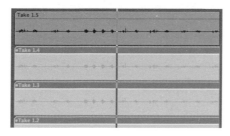

Figure 4.22

Selecting 'Takes'

Once you have a series of Takes you'll want to choose the best bits and compile them onto one track – the 'Comp'.

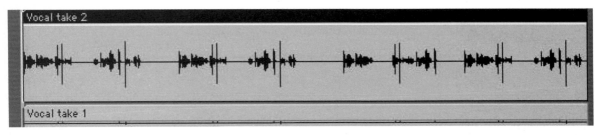

Figure 4.23

First, name each Take to 'Take 1', 'Take 2' and so on. De-Mute the Regions. To keep easy track of each Take, it's a good idea to give them different colours. To do this, select a Take and select Colors from the View menu (Fiure 4.24). A colour picker window opens (Figure 4.25). Choose a colour. Now select another Take and choose another colour (Figure 4.26). Repeat this until all Takes are coloured differently. Close the Color window.

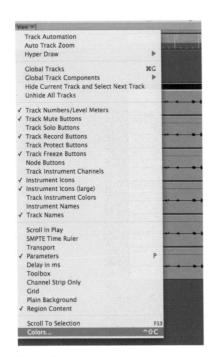

Figure 4.24

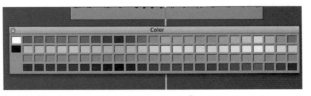

Figure 4.25

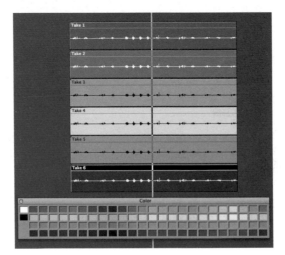

Figure 4.26

Use the scissors tool (or the Strip Silence as described earlier in the Chapter) to cut each Take into Regions. These might be a phrase from a Vocal or a Guitar Lick.

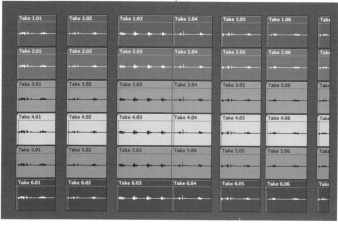

Figure 4.27

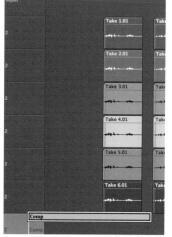

Figure 4.28

Create a new Audio Track at the bottom of the Takes. Make sure all Tracks the Takes are on and this Track are the same (in this case It's Audio 2). Make sure the View menu Instrument name item is checked and call the Track 'Comp'.

Now audition each Region. Use the Solo and Mute buttons to listen to Regions individually. Drag any Regions you like to the lower 'Comp' Track. The Lowest tracks always mutes any of the same Tracks above so you'll only hear the 'Comp' Track.

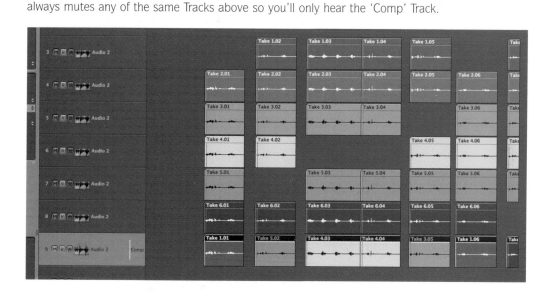

Figure 4.29

Figure 4.30

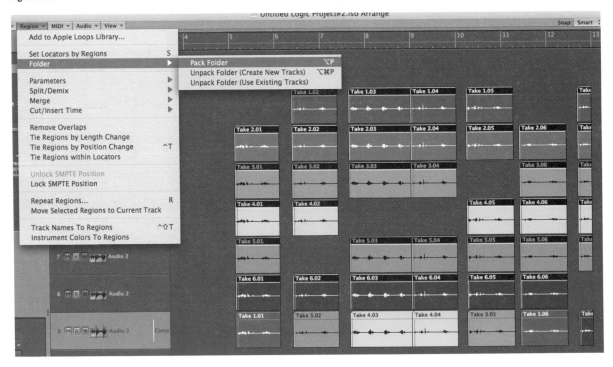

Figure 4.31

Drum editing using folders

If you are recording acoustic drums, it's likely that you'll have several tracks worth of recordings for bass drum, snare, hi-hats and so on. A typical drum recording could look like the figure on the next page.

Figure 4.32

You may want to split these drum recordings into sections, such as 'verse', 'chorus', middle eight' and so on so you can move these around to experiment with different arrangements. In the following figure, Markers have been created showing the different sections of the song. To create drum parts representing these sections, you could just split all the channels and drag these around.

Figure 4.33

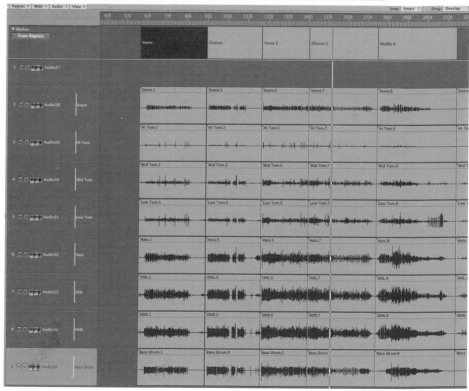

Tip

You can use several Folder-related Key Commands to navigate into and out of Folders.

But it's easy to get confused with so many tracks and you may find that you leave behind a recording when you copy and drag, or accidentally erase a recording altogether. It'd be much easier if you could just cut and paste a single track, which would affect all the drums together. We can do this in Logic using Folders.

First select all the drum recordings.

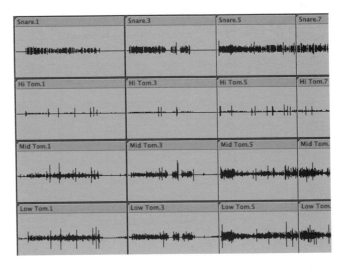

Figure 4.34

Now choose the Arrange page menu item Region>Folder>Pack folder to create a Folder with all the drum recordings in it.

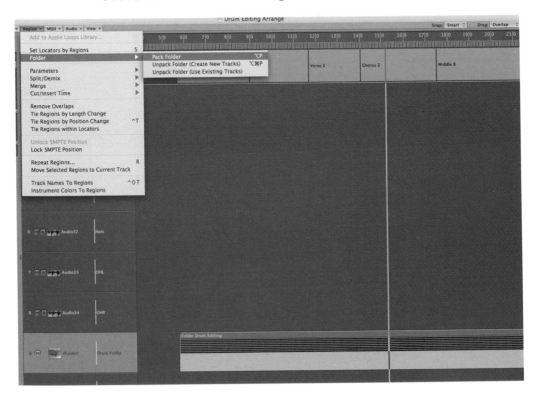

Figure 4.35

If you double click on the Folder you can see all the drum recordings. To close the Folder click on the box at the top left of the window.
Now you can cut and rename the folder as you please.

Figure 4.36

Figure 4.37

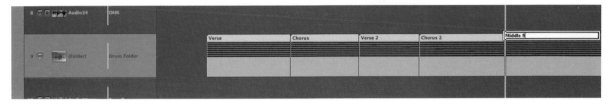

Use the text Tool and click on each Region to rename them or select and rename in the Region Parameter box.

Tip

Use the Goto next/Previous marker Key Commands to easily navigate Markers.

Figure 4.38   Figure 4.39

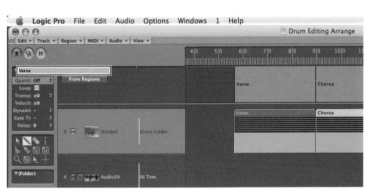

Each section can then be dragged around to create new arrangements.

Figure 4.40

As drums are real instruments, cymbal crashes and other sustained sounds can overlap sections. You may have to go into a Folder and extend the shortened Regions to stop this happening.

Figure 4.41

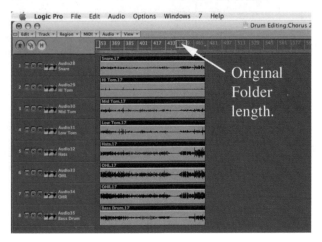

Original Folder length.

Then extend the length of the Folder by dragging the length box.

Figure 4.42

Tip

You can return any recorded audio Regions to their original position using the Arrange Page>Audio>Move Regions to Original Record Position.

Double-click on a Folder to see its contents.

You can, of course, use this method for any instrument that has been recorded using multiple microphones, or, indeed, whole recordings.

MIDI Recording

Capture last take

Tip

The 'Capture last take' command doesn't work when recording audio. You need to press record first!

As far as MIDI is concerned, Logic is always in record. So if Logic is playing, you can capture any MIDI recording (and this includes Virtual instruments) using the 'Capture last take' Key Command.

Extended Region parameters

While the standard Region Parameter box has most of the quantize parameters you'll need when editing Regions, there are times when finer control is required. For this you can use the Extended Region Parameter box, which is opened from the Option menu or a Key Command.

Figure 4.43

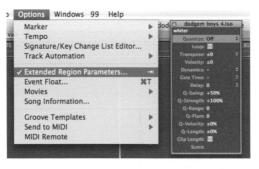

Figure 4.44

The extra parameters are as follows

- Q-Swing. This % value alters the position of every second point in the quantization grid. Use settings between 50% and 75% to give your quantization a 'swing' feel.
- Q-Strength. This determines how far a note is shifted towards the nearest quantize grid position. 100% is full quantization, 0% is no quantization.
- Q-Range. All notes, whose distance from the nearest quantize grid position is the number of ticks set here, are not quantized. A value of 0 means every note is quantized. If you enter negative values (Far Quantize) only notes outside the

selected Region are quantized. Use this to bring the worst played notes in a Region into time. If you enter positive values (Linear quantize) notes that are more 'laid back' that the rest of the Region are brought into line. This value is connected to the Q-strength setting

- Q-Flam. Chords get spread out by this parameter. Positive values produce an upwards arpeggio, negative values a downward one. The first note is unaltered.
- Q-Velocity. This parameter affects how much the velocity values of the Region are affected by velocity values in a Groove Template. At 0% the velocity is unaltered. At 100% it takes on the velocity values of the Groove template. Negative values make the deviation more extreme.
- Q-Length. This is similar to Q-Velocity but affects the note lengths in the Region. 0% has no effect, ie the note lengths are unchanged. 100% means the note lengths become the same as the those in the template. negative values make the deviation more extreme.
- Clip Length. When this is on, any note stretching past the end of a Region will be cut off. This is a playback parameter only. The original note length remains unchanged.

MIDI (and Virtual instrument) Multi-Track recording

You can record several MIDI tracks together all at the same time. If you have a keyboard player, MIDI guitar and drums, you can get a 'band' feel yet still have the luxury of editing notes and beats after the recording. Or you can just layer multiple MIDI or Virtual instruments all played at the same time.

These two types of Multi-track MIDI recording, selected from the File>Song Settings>Recording menu

- File>Song Settings>Recording>Audo Demix by Channel if Multitrack recording is ON

Figure 4.45

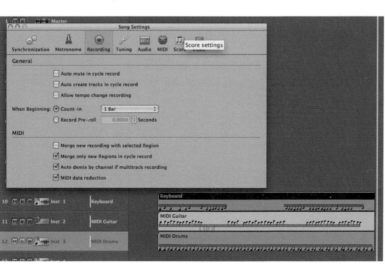

Figure 4.46

This is MultiPlayer recording. If you have different MIDI controllers, say MIDI Keyboard, Guitar and Drum pads, they will all be recorded onto separate Regions on the record enabled tracks

Figure 4.47

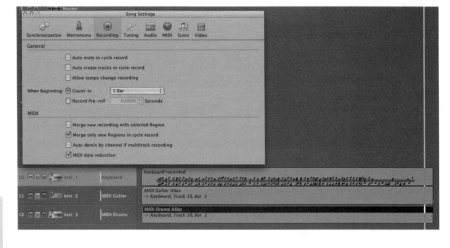

Figure 4.48

- File>Song Settings>Recording>Audo Demix by Channel if Multitrack recording is OFF

This is Layer recording. In this mode, only one Region is recorded (on the selected Instrument track). The other recorded instruments just have aliases of the one recording.

Using Virtual instruments

Using Multi-timbral Virtual Instruments

Some Virtual instruments can respond to more than one MIDI channel at a time – just like old school hardware multi-timbral boxes. You might want MIDI channel 1 to control a bass sound, channel 2 a piano, channel 10 drums and so on. This is how you can do it in Logic.

Insert the Multi-timbral Virtual instrument in an Instrument object. In this case it's Instrument 1. Make sure each sound is set to receive on individual MIDI channels.

Figure 4.49

Open the Environment and create a new page. Rename it something useful – in this case it's the Garritan Personal Orchestra (GPO), which can receive MIDI and play back different sounds on up to 8 MIDI channels.

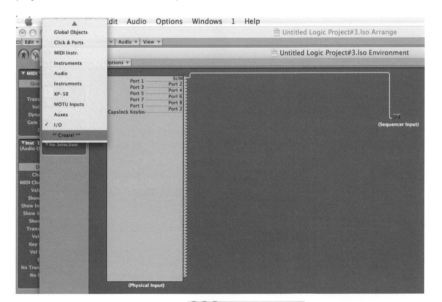

Figure 4.50

Figure 4.51

Figure 4.52

Create a Multi Instrument object from the from the Environment page New menu.

Figure 4.53

Figure 4.54

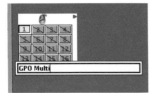

Rename the Multi Instrument to something useful. Click on the box with a '1' in it. Make sure the box next to the Icon is ticked so the Instrument shows up in the Arrange page. Now repeat this for the other 7 channels.

Figure 4.55

Figure 4.56

Hold down the Option key and click on the little arrow at the top right of the Multi Instrument and cable it to the GPO Virtual Instrument on Instrument 1. When Logic asks you if you want to change the Cable and Channel Port, choose 'remove'.

Figure 4.57

Figure 4.58

Figure 4.59

Now, each of these individual channels is available in the Arrange page. Selecting 'GPO channel 1' will play back the sound assigned to MIDI channel 1 on the GPO, 'GPO channel 1' will play MIDI channel 1 and so on.

Figure 4.60

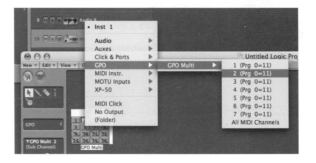

You could also use single channel MIDI Instruments (Environment page>New menu). Create one; give it the required MIDI channel, rename it and cable it to the GPO Instrument (Hold down the Option Key and click on the arrow as above). Note the little stubby cable showing that the Instrument is cabled to another Layer in the Environment.

Figure 4.61

You then need to make 6 more Instruments. You can copy object by dragging them while holding down the Option key. Don't forget to change their MIDI channels. Note the little stubby cable showing that the Instrument is cabled to another Layer in the Environment

These can then be chosen in the Arrange page in the same ways as for the Multi Instrument.

Figure 4.62

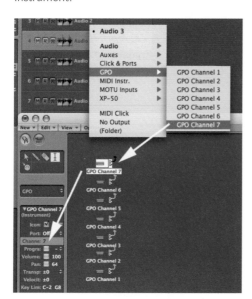

Figure 4.63

Using Multi-timbral Virtual Instruments without Multiple outputs

If you have a multi-timbral Virtual instrument that doesn't have separate outputs for each of it's sounds, but you wish to process each sound assigned to each MIDI channel in a different way, use a different instance of the Virtual instrument for each channel and load a different sound into each. In the figure below, there are 8 GPO instances each with different sounds loaded.

Figure 4.64

Multi output (Multi channel) Virtual instruments

Some Virtual instruments Including Logic's own Ultrabeat and EXS24 can be used in their multiple output versions.

Figure 4.65

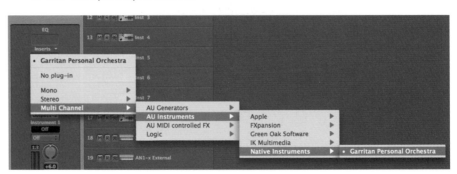

What this means in practice is that you can send individual sounds from these instruments to Aux objects and process these sounds further with plug-ins. Here's how you set this up using Ultrabeat as an example.

Instance the Multi channel version of Ultrabeat on an Instrument object – it's Instrument 4 in this example.

Figure 4.66

Open the Environment and create a new page – call it 'Ultrabeat multi out.'

Figure 4.67

Create a new Audio instrument from the New menu and double click on it to make it full size. Highlight it and select an Aux from the Channel pull down menu. Rename the object something like 'Ultrabeat output 1'. Make sure it's set to a mono channel.

If you click on the box next to 'I/O' on the object, you'll see a pull down menu appear. Choose 'Ultrabeat' 3 from the menu. Outputs 1 and 2 will always come out of the main Instrument object.

Hold down the Option key and drag to copy the Audio object. Highlight the second object and select the next Aux from the Channel menu. It's important you do this before you perform the next actions.

Figure 4.69

Figure 4.68

Figure 4.70

Rename the new Aux to 'Ultrabeat output 2'

Figure 4.71

Figure 4.72

Click on the box next to 'I/O' on the object. Choose 'Ultrabeat' 4 from the pull down menu.

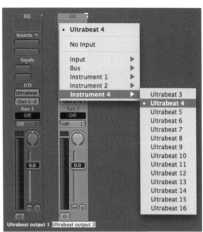

Repeat until you have 14 objects, renaming then 'Ultrabeat 3', 'Ultrabeat 4' and so on. (Ultrabeat has 16 outputs – 2 on the Instrument channel the plug-in is inserted on and 14 here). Now you can add plug-in effects to each of these channels and adjust individual pan and volume settings.

Figure 4.73

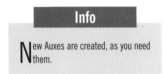

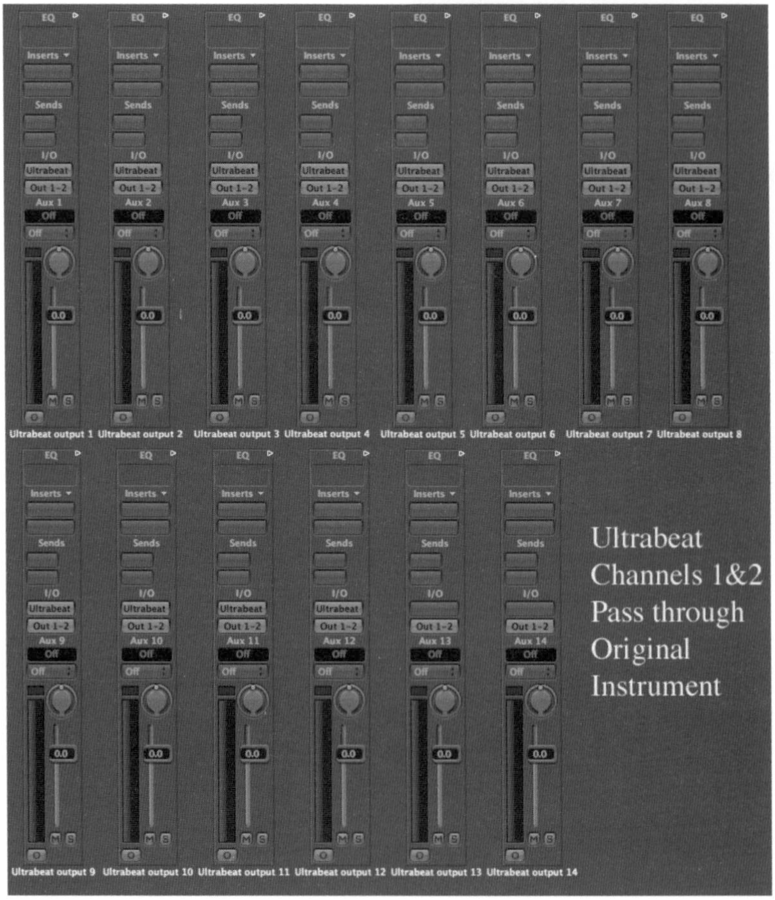

Info

New Auxes are created, as you need them.

Tip

Use stereo Auxes for stereo outputs.

Figure 4.74

General recording tips

Aliases of MIDI Regions

You can make Aliases of MIDI Regions on the Arrange page. These are useful if you want to make sure that if you edit a Region any copies of that Region will also change. You create Aliases of a MIDI Region by selecting it and using the MIDI>Alias>Make menu item. You can turn an Alias into a real copy (and therefore edit it separately from the original Region), from the same menu.

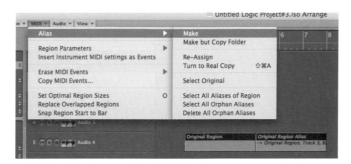

Figure 4.75

Looping Regions

You can loop any Region in two ways.

If you highlight the Region to be looped and click the Loop box on the Region parameter box, the Region will be looped until the end of the song or until another Region is encountered.

Info

Looping in this context isn't the same as using Apple Loops. More on these in Chapter 8.

Figure 4.76

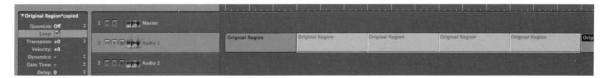

If you drag the Region's top right corner the mouse pointer turns into a Looping tool. Dragging with this tool will loop the Region as far as you drag with the mouse. As you can see, you can choose where to end the loop.

Figure 4.77

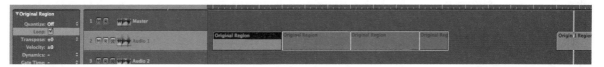

Audio File formats

Logic can Import and bounce down to, several different file formats. Which of these you need to use depends on the project. Here are some tips on which format to use.

Info

The default file type is set in the Audio Preferences window.

AIFF

These are non-compressed files and are the 'standard' audio file used with the Macintosh – though they can be read on Windows machines too. It's usual for the default recording file type in Logic to be set to AIFF. AIFF files can be 16 or 24 bit and any sample rate up to Logic's maximum. When bouncing, AIFF files can be read by most Mastering studios and the files are widely transferable across Macintosh audio software.

WAV

WAV files are the standard file type of the Windows PC. You may want to set the Logic default file type to WAV if you are exchanging data between your Mac and a Windows version of Logic. WAV files can be 16 or 24 bit and any sample rate up to Logic's maximum. When bouncing, you may want to use a WAV format if you want to master on a Windows machine or you are sending a mixdown to be used on a PC-based video editing program.

MP3

This is a compressed audio format; that is, data is discarded to make the file size smaller. MP3 is the file type of choice if you want to e-mail your mixdowns or make your songs available for download. MP3's can be bounced at varying qualities – the better the quality, the bigger the file.

AAC

This is Apple's own compressed format. It's similar in many ways to MP3, but arguably of better quality. Use this format for exporting into iTunes.

SDII

This is the full bandwidth file type of Digidesign's Pro Tools. SDII files can be 16 or 24 bit and any sample rate up to Logic's maximum You may want to use this as Logic's default file type if you will want to exchange Songs with Pro Tools users – though, these days, Pro Tools can also work with AIFF. Some Video editing houses, especially those working with Avid systems, use SDII files.

Tip

If you are sending files of mixdowns to be mastered or for use in a film or video, you need to make sure you send the correct format. You may also want to use the ISO 9660 CD Burning format and send the files as data rather than Audio to maintain compatibility and quality.

Sample rates

The Sample rate you can use for recording in Logic is defined by the capabilities of your Audio interface. The default recording rate is set either in your hardware's supplied software or the Audio MIDI setup application located in the Applications/Utilities folder.

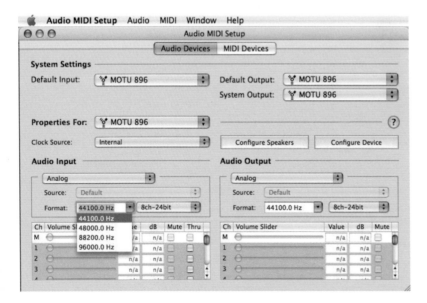

Figure 4.78

Or in the Audio>Sample Rate menu (right).

Higher sample rates yield higher recording quality. The highest frequency you can record is half that of the sample rate. So 44.1kHz can record up to 22.5kHz - just outside the human hearing range. 96kHz can record up to 48kHz. However there is a price to pay; higher sample rates require more hard disk space required to store the file and more CPU power to process. Also, if you plan finally to release your material on CD, that format is limited to 44.1kHz – and sample rate conversion is not without quality problems. Higher sampling rates do produce better quality recordings; though if you are record- ing only electronic music you may not notice the difference. You'll also need higher quality ancillary equipment, especially monitoring, to hear the subtle improvements of the higher sample rates.

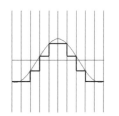

Figure 4.79

Figure 4.80 (Low sampling rate)   Figure 4.81 (High sampling rate)

- Use a sample rate of 44.1kHz if you plan to release on audio CD.
- Use a sample rate of 48kHz if you are producing audio for DVD. This is the default DVD sampling rate for audio.
- Use a higher sample rate if you are recording acoustic sessions or want to release on a higher resolution format such as SACD.

Info

Logic performs automatic real-time sample rate conversion. If a project was recorded using a sample rate your Audio hardware does not support, it will be converted to one that it does support.

Bit level

The bit level used in recording defines the resolution and quality of a recording. The lower the bit level used, the less well an analog signal will be reproduced, as the recording will use less steps to digitize the sound.

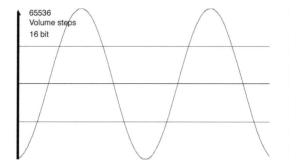

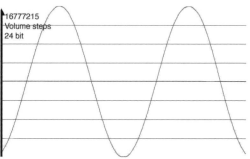

CD is 16 bit and it describes 65535 discrete level values. A 4 bit recording sys- tem will only have 256. You can look at bit depth in the same way as resolution on a digital camera – the higher the bit depth the more 'in focus' the sound. In audio terms, the bit depth defines the dynamic range, measured in dB.

Figure 4.82 (left)
16 bit resolution

Figure 4.83 (right)
24 bit resolution

You can measure the dynamic range that will be given by a bit depth using the formula 6 x the number of bits

So a 16 bit system has a dynamic range of 6 x 16 = 96dB
Whereas a 4 bit system only has a dynamic range of 6 x 4 = 24dB

As you can see from the figures above, the greater the bit rate, the more discrete amplitude steps are described by the digitised waveform.

0dB

In analog recordings, it was common to push a recording level 'into the red' – i.e. over the 0dB meter mark. In an analog tape recorder, preamplifier, compressor or mixing desk, the distortion or saturation that occurs when you do this is pleasing to the ear. This is one of the reasons that some engineers swear by analog recording – the saturation is often used as an effect. In the digital domain things are very different. You should never record an input at a level over 0dB on your input meter, or have any playback channel or master output meter pass this limit. The distortion in digital systems when you do this isn't pleasant; unless you're actually trying to make unpleasant noises that is!

Monitoring

When you record into Logic there are a few requirements everyone will need.

- To be able to hear what you are recording
- To be able to hear what has previously been recorded
- To be able to monitor effects – but not necessarily record them
- To be able to replace sections that were badly played or sung.

In all these situations you'll need to hear or 'monitor' what you are doing. There are several ways to do this in Logic.

Software monitoring

This is turned on from Logic's Audio Preferences>Drivers window.

When this is set to 'ON' the audio path through Logic is as detailed in Figure 4.85.

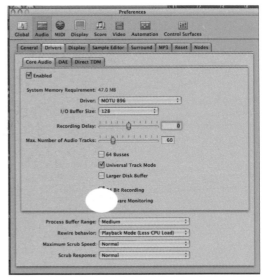

Figure 4.84

Figure 4.85

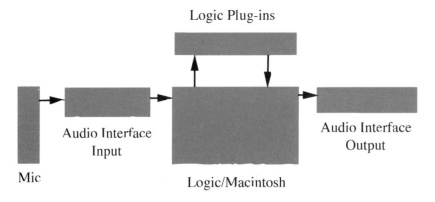

Logic Plug-ins

Audio Interface
Input

Audio Interface
Output

Mic

Logic/Macintosh

As you can see, the audio passing through Logic is subject to the latency in the system, as it takes time to pass through all the stages, so you may want to check out the section covering latency earlier in this chapter.

The advantage of software monitoring is that you can apply monitoring-only effects to the recording channel. For example, its nice for a vocalist to hear a bit of reverb while singing, but record the vocals dry.

Hardware monitoring

If you turn software monitoring to 'off' you won't have as much of a latency problem, but you won't be able to add a software reverb plug-in to the recording Audio object. You can get around this by using a mixer and an external reverb – as shown in Figure 4.86.

Figure 4.86

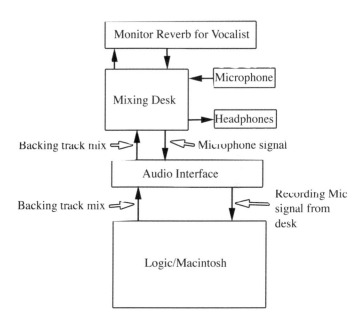

Monitor Reverb for Vocalist

Mixing Desk

Microphone

Headphones

Backing track mix

Microphone signal

Audio Interface

Backing track mix

Recording Mic
signal from
desk

Logic/Macintosh

Info

Some Audio interfaces have a direct monitoring feature that sends the audio from the input directly to the output thus eliminating latency. The same caveats as for Software monitoring being set to OFF apply to these as well.

Punching in

In the old tape-based recording days, where tracks were limited, an engineer would often replace mistakes by 'punching-in'. This entailed rewinding the tape to a position before the mistake, pressing play and then record exactly at the right point. Even a slight error could mean that good material before and after the punch-in could be lost. You can emulate this technique in Logic using the locators and the punch-in button on the Transport bar, but as we now effectively have an unlimited amount of tracks, there's a much easier way to perform the same operation.

First locate the section of the recording that you want to replace. Use the Scissors tool, Marquee tool or the 'Split Regions/Events by Song Position' Key Command.

Figure 4.87

Delete the offending Region.

Create another Audio Track under the old recording. Select the Track.

Figure 4.88

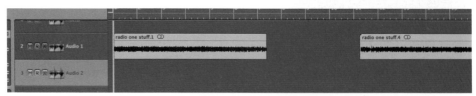

Figure 4.89

Record the new material onto this new Track. You'll be able to hear the old recording up to the error.

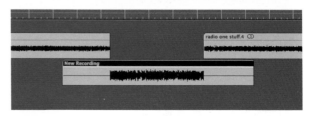

Figure 4.90

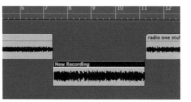

Drag the ends of the new recording so they line up with the gaps on the original recording Track.

Drag the Region into the gap.

Figure 4.91

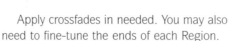

Apply crossfades in needed. You may also need to fine-tune the ends of each Region.

Figure 4.92

Crossfades

When you cut up audio files and butt discontinuous Regions up against each other, you'll often get a click or a level change as the SPL plays over the join. To cure this problem, you'll need to use crossfades.

Select the crossfade tool from the Toolbox.

Figure 4.93

Drag it over the join. You'll see the fade being drawn.

You can change the slope and type of the fade in the Parameter box. You may only need very small values to clear up a click. Too high a value may sound like a fade out.

Figure 4.94

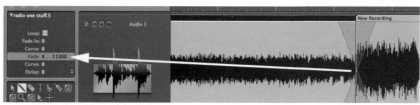

Figure 4.95

Curved crossfades often sound more natural than a simple 'X' shape fade.

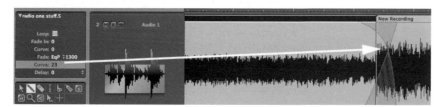

Figure 4.96

If there is a discontinuity between the Regions, use Volume Automation to adjust the levels.

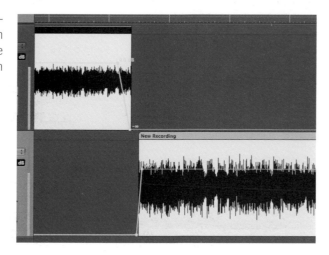

Figure 4.97

Figure 4.98

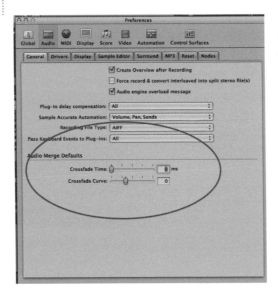

The default crossfade values are foung in the general Audio Preferences window.

Tempo tips

Most recording people do these days is done to a strict tempo. However, if you are recording 'real' musicians, or you've recorded something with spur of the moment inspiration, you may still want to perform quantizing or tempo editing on the data. For this you'll need to get Logic to understand the Tempo of your recording.

Using the computer keyboard set the tempo

Say, for example you have pre-recorded music on tape and you want to set the tempo of Logic Pro to the same tempo. You can use a computer keyboard key to enter this tempo.

Using the tempo interpreter

Figure 4.99

Assign the Key Command Tap tempo in the Key Commands window to a suitable computer key.

Put Logic into manual sync mode from the menu on the Transport bar and open the Tempo interpreter from the list.

Figure 4.100

You can set the following parameter values:

- Tap step - Sets the note value that the taps will be describing. Best results will be obtained by using larger values. Try 1/4 note to start.

- Window(Ticks) - Sets a window within which incoming taps are used. Taps outside this window are ignored. The narrower the window you can use, the better.
- Tempo response - This adjusts the sensitivity to tempo changes. The larger the values the greater the sensitivity. Start with 4.
- Max Tempo change - Sets the maximum tempo change possible. Select as small a value as possible to reduce the tempo fluctuations to a minimum.
- Tap Count-in - Logic starts responding to incoming taps after this count-in period has passed.
- Smoothing - When on, smoothes out large changes in the incoming tempo.
- Tempo recording - When on, a tempo list is created as you tap.
- Pre   Displays all the incoming taps
- Post   Displays only taps that fall in the above set parameters

Close the tap tempo windows. Now start tapping on the key you set up in the Key Command window. After the count-in, Logic Pro will start at the tempo of the tapping. The tempo determined is displayed in the Transport bar.

Beat Mapping and the Global Track

This allows you to set the tempo of a song after recording, allowing you to play freely and worry about the tempo afterwards. Once you have 'beat mapped' the recording, you'll get all the advantages of recording with a metronome, such as;

- The metronome click will be in time
- You can quantize Regions
- MIDI and Apple loops will automatically adjust to the tempo of the song.
- It helps with interpretation in the Score editor.

When using beat mapping you correct the beats present in your recording to the bar positions on the Beat mapping Track window. Here are a couple of examples.

Select the beat mapping Global Track from the Arrange Page View>Global Tracks components menu.

Make sure the Global Track is visible from the same View menu.

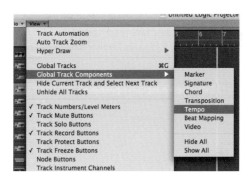

Figure 4.101

Figure 4.102

MIDI or Virtual instrument Regions

Record a Region without using the Metronome. Note that the initial tempo set in Logic is 120 bpm (beats per minute). If you open the Matrix editor, you can see where the beats actually lie in the performance (Figure 4.103).

You can see where Logic has displayed the actual notes in the part on the Beat Mapping Global track in Figure 4.104.

Figure 4.103 (left)

Figure 4.104 (right)

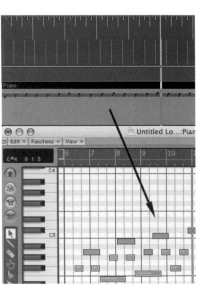

The next part can be performed in either the Matrix editor or Arrange page (or Hyper editor, for that matter). Select the first note in the Region.

Figure 4.105

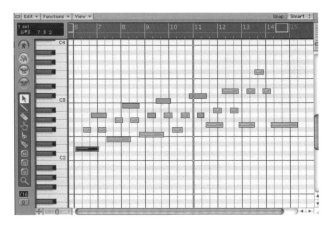

Click and hold on the first beat in the Beat mapping track. You'll see that the line will turn yellow and that 'Set Beat' will appear in a small window.

Drag the mouse (while still holding down the mouse key to the first note in the Region.) Release the mouse key. You'll see that the first note in the Region is aligned to the first note of the bar in the Beat mapping track.

Figure 4.106 (left)

Figure 4.107 (right)

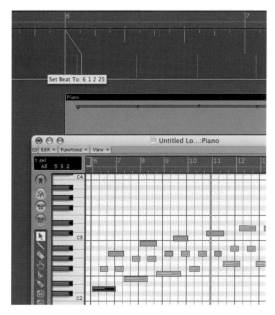

Now select the note that you consider to be the first in the next bar.

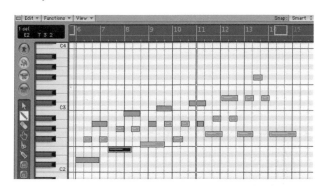

Figure 4.108

Click and drag the yellow line from the bar line to the note in the same way as for the first bar.

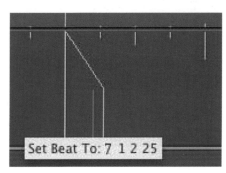

Figure 4.109

Release the mouse key. You'll see that the second note selected in the Region is aligned to the second bar of Beat mapping track.

Figure 4.110

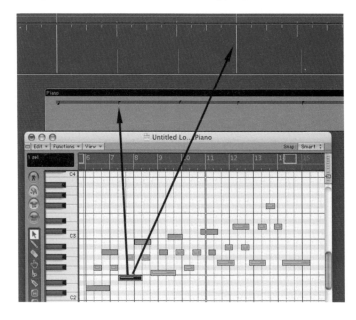

Repeat for all the bars in the Region (this Region has 4 bars of playing). Now repeat for any notes within the bar if needed. Logic will create tempo changes for each bar – you can see these if you open the Tempo Global Track.

Figure 4.111

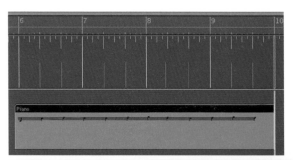

If you just set the tempo for the first bar or a Region, you can then quantize the entire Region using this tempo value as a guide. To delete set tempo points, click using the erase tool.

Figure 4.112

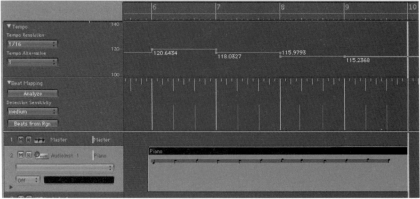

Audio Regions

To map an audio Region. Logic must determine rhythmically significant spots in the recording. For a drum snippet, this could be the bass drum or hi-hat part. These spots are usually louder or more prominent and Logic can use this to analyse the recording.

Select an audio Region. This is a 4 bar drum loop.

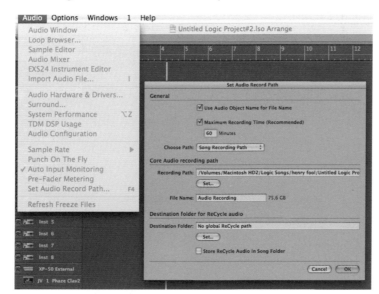

Figure 4.113

Figure 4.114

Click on Analyze to detect the transients in the Audio file.

There are a couple of parameters you may like to consider when trying to use Beat mapping with audio Regions.

Detection sensitivity

A high detection sensitivity will detect more transients and give you more points in which to use for Beat Mapping. This may or may not be a good thing, depending on the audio Region – you may detect transients that are not really there.

Like a lot of things in Logic, you can always undo the Beat detection and retry at any time.

Start with a low detection sensitivity and increase the value until you get the results you require.

Once you have detected the transients, you can Beat map the tempo in exactly the same way as for MIDI Regions.

If you record a MIDI Region (using an external sound source or Virtual instrument) with a Metronome, you can use the

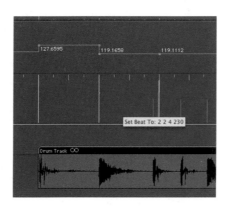

Figure 4.115

Beats from Region button to 'map' the tempo from this MIDI Region to the song.

Record a Region with a fixed tempo close to the one of the audio file. Edit the beats in the Region until they sync with the audio file beats. Then click the Beats from Region button. Logic will create tempo changes to preserve the timing.

Figure 4.116

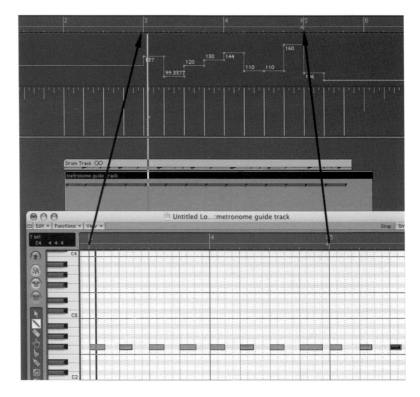

Lock SMPTE position

If you're working to picture, there'll probably be times you'll want to make sure some Regions are locked into position even if you change the Tempo. You can make sure they stay put whatever you do to the Temp from the Region>Lock/Unlock Tempo Position menu items. It's handy to set these up as Key Commands too.

Track protection

You can prevent the accidental change or deletion of a Track by using the Track protect buttons. These can be made visible on the Arrange page from the View>Track protect buttons menu item.

Figure 4.117

Plug-ins

Logic Audio Units

Logic used the Audio Unit (AU) standard for plug-ins introduced by Apple with OSX. AU plug-ins are located in the Library/Audio/Plug-ins/Components folder and are loaded when Logic boots. You might want to check out Logic's AU manager in Chapter 1 as AU plug-in verification is a common cause of problems.

Apple's Audio Unit plug-ins

Apple ship several useful plug-ins, which can be found in the Audio Unit pull down menu – so they are often missed. Don't ignore these though. They may look pretty simple but some of them are extremely useful (Figure 5.1).

Figure 5.1 (left)
Apple plug-ins in the Audio units folder

Figure 5.2
AUMatrixReverb

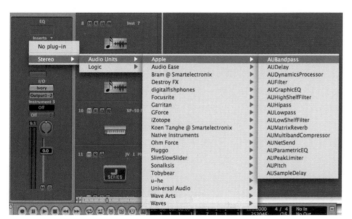

AUMatrixReverb is a fine sounding reverb unit (Figure 5.2). It's probably an improvement on Logic's Platinumverb, although the Space Designer outclasses it – but then again, it uses a lot less CPU resources.

AUPitch uses OSX 10.4.x's pitch changing algorithms to smoothly change the pitch of audio files. It produces a much better result than the Sample editor's Time Machine. The algorithms are also available in the Arrange page when using the 'fit

Figure 5.3
AUPitch

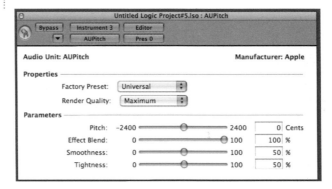

to the bar' feature (Figure 5.3). See Chapter 7 for more on this.

AUNetSend and AUNetReceive

These two operate as a pair. You can use AUNetSend to send audio over a network (using 'Bonjour') and receive the Audio on another Mac running AUNetReceive.

Figure 5.4
AUPitch

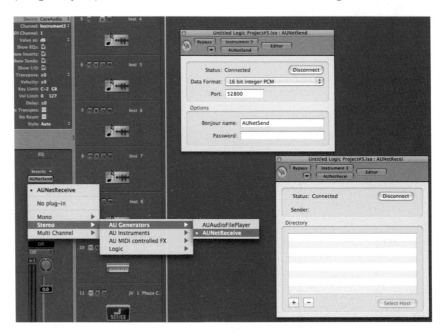

Here's how you do it. Load AUNetSend on the first Mac. In this example, it's instanced on a Piano sound in Logic. If you then load AUNetReceive on the second Mac, it will pick up the AUNetSend on the first Mac – assuming they are both networked together (Figures 5.5 and 5.6).

Figure 5.5 (left)
Figure 5.6

Playing the piano plug-in on the first Mac will sound through the second Mac. You can send any audio this way, at a variety of quality levels (Figure 5.7). If you find that you can't connect AUNetSend to AUNetReceive try switching off the Firewall in the System Preferences Sharing window (Figure 5.8).

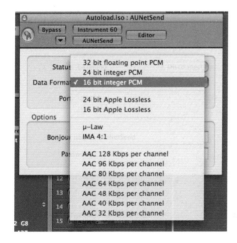

Figure 5.7 (above)

Figure 5.8

GarageBand instruments

Logic comes with the full range of Virtual instruments that is supplied with GarageBand – ostensibly for GarageBand compatibility. These are simplified versions of Logic's own plug-ins, but again, don't ignore them. They are just as fine sounding and their simplified interfaces lend themselves to rapid experimentation.

Figure 5.9

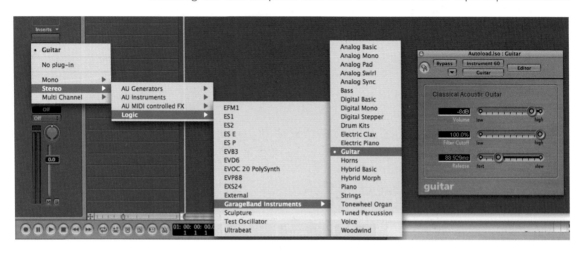

Using VST plug-ins in Logic

Although Logic itself cannot use VST plug-ins directly, it's AU only, you can circumvent this limitation with some third-party software. These so-called VST 'wrappers' create a shell that fools Logic into believing it is loading an AU plug-in.

Figure 5.3
AUPitch

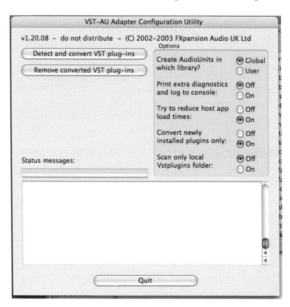

Third-party plug-ins in Logic

While Logic has a plug-in to suit most occasions, there will always be times when you want to use a particular synthesizer, compressor or EQ. Logic supports third-party AU plug-ins. Usually these are installed automatically when you run the plug-in installer program, but occasionally you have to install them yourself.

AU plug-ins are stored in the Library/Audio/Plug-ins/Components folder. If your third-party AU plug-in doesn't appear in the Object list, make sure it's not been disabled by Logic's AU manager. See chapter 1 for more on this.

Effects plug-ins

The Helper menu has several plug-ins that aren't immediately obvious in their functions.

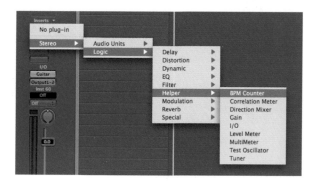

Figure 5.11 (left)
Helper plug-ins

Figure 5.12
BPM counter

BPM Counter

This can detect the tempo of a recording when inserted on the Track it is playing on. It's useful if you have some drum loops and you don't know the tempo, for example.

Correlation meter

This meter helps you to check if your recordings will be mono-compatible – very useful for TV and radio work. If the meter is reading positive, the more mono compatible your recording is. If it's negative, there will be phase cancellations when the Song is played in mono.

Figure 5.13 (below)
Correlation meter

Direction mixer

This is a sophisticated Pan controller that can also deal with MS (Middle and Side) encoded audio. As you turn the DirMixer direction control to the right the signal will pan towards the right – it's hard right at 90 degrees. As you continue turning the control clockwise, the signal will appear to swap channels – almost as if the signal is being panned around in a circle. The Basis control sets the width of this spread. A value of 0 gives a mono signal. When the value is greater than 1, the signal appears to come from outside the speakers, which is useful for ambient effects.

Figure 5.14 (below)
Direction mixer

Gain

This plug-in allows you to increase the gain of any signal, along with left/right balance. It's useful if you have something recorded at a really low level or a plug-in instrument that has a low output level. You could also use it to match levels between plug-ins instanced on the same Track.

If you insert a Gain plug-in on the Master output track, you can use it to check out playback in mono.

You can invert the phase of the left and/or right channel signal to create a wide special effect. It's also useful when you have Tracks recorded with microphones that have phase problems.

Figure 5.16
Gain plug-in

Figure 5.17
I/O plug-in

I/O

This plug-in allows you to route audio into and out of Logic via the physical inputs and outputs of your Audio interface. You choose the required channel from the Input and Output pull down menus – how many are there depends on your interface. You can adjust the input and output levels. Use this plug-in to send and return to a hardware effects unit (such as a reverb) so it can be used in-line with plug-in effects.

Level meter

This is a high-resolution level meter. Insert this on the Master output to get a better picture of your levels. You can choose from 3 different modes for the meter. Peak shows the maximum level wit a hold function so you can see what's going on over a whole song. RMS shows the average level. Peak & RMS combines the two modes.

Figure 5.18
Level meter plug-in

Multimeter

In Analyser mode, this plug-in shows a real-time graphic display of the frequency range of a signal. You can use it on whole mixes to see what the spectral balance of your mix is like and compare it with commercial releases.

In Goniometer mode, the plug-in helps you see any phase problems in a stereo signal. If you get signal cancellations along the M line, you have phase problems – something is canceling out in the centre signal.

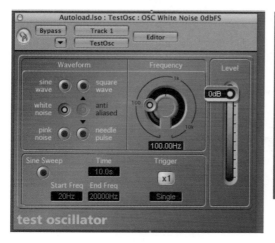

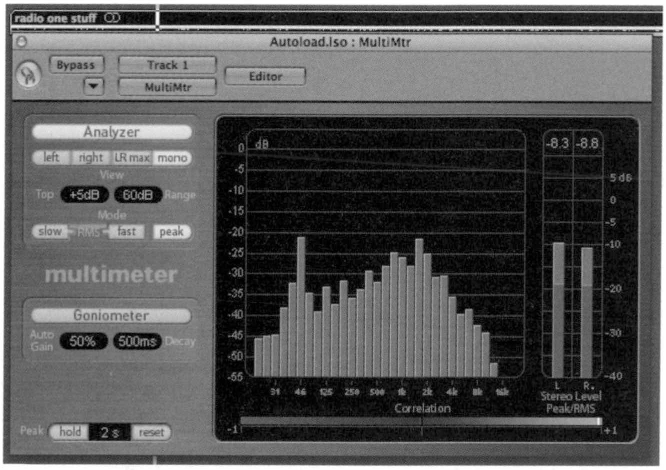

Figure 5.3
Multimeter plug-in

The multimeter also has a Correlation meter (see above)

Test Oscillator

Mainly designed to help produce impulse responses for Space Designer, you can also use it as a sine wave effects generator. Try using it as a side chain input to the Ring Modulator plug-in. When inserted on a on an Audio Track, Logic must be playing for the oscillator to work.

Tuner

This is a handy chromatic tuner. Insert it onto a recording Track and use it to tune a guitar.

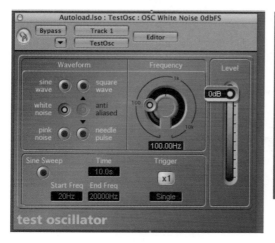

Figure 5.21 (left)
Test oscillator

Figure 5.22
Chromatic tuner

Special menu

The Special menu has several plug-ins that aren't immediately obvious in their functions.

Enhanced Timer

This plug-in allows you to quantize audio in a similar fashion to MIDI data. It's a simple plug-in. Choose the grid you want to quantize to and adjust the slider until you get the desired effect. This plug-in works only if it's inserted in the first slot on a channel.

Figure 5.23
Enhanced Timer plug-in

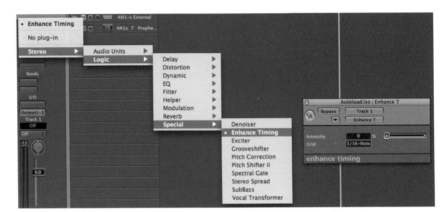

Pitch Correction

This plug-in attempts to bring out of tune audio back into tune in real-time.

- This plug-in can help with correcting minor deviations from pitch (shown on the 'keyboard' display).
- The faster the response setting, the more likely you'll hear artifacts. These can be used creatively as many a hit record will testify!
- Choose the range of the signal to be corrected. Low for bass sounds, such as Fretless Bass. Choose Normal for those with high frequency content, such as vocals.
- Choose a scale and root note if you can.
- You can bypass certain notes from the correction process.

Figure 5.24
Pitch correction plug-in

You can automate the pitch correction plug-in parameters to get the right settings for different parts of a song, and you can use the Apple AUPitch plug-in to process individual notes that are out of tune.

• Isolate the offending note and split it from the surrounding region using the Marquee tool

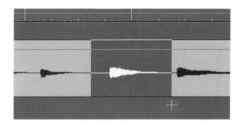

Figure 5.25
Isolate the offending note

• Drag it to another Track. Convert it to an independent audio file using the Arrange page>Audio>Convert Regions to New audio files. Insert the AUPitch plug-in on the Track.

Figure 5.26
Drag it to another Track

• Adjust the offending Region. You may want to loop around a wider section of the Song to hear it in context. Select the Region and export it using the File>Export>Export Region as Audio file. Make sure the 'Add resulting files to Audio Window' is set.

Figure 5.27
Adjust the offending Region

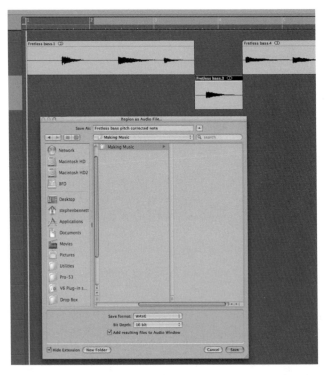

- Open the Audio window; Drag the processed Region to the gap in the original Track.
- Mute the processed Region.

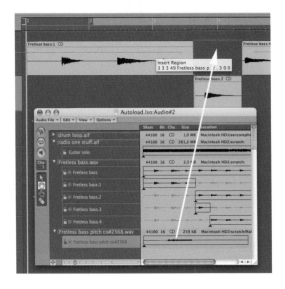

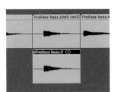

Figure 5.28 (left)
Drag the processed Region to the gap

Figure 5.29 (above)
Mute the processed Region

Channel EQ and Linear Phase EQ

At first glance, these two EQs may look very similar and, in fact, you can copy presets between them. However, sonically, they are quite different.

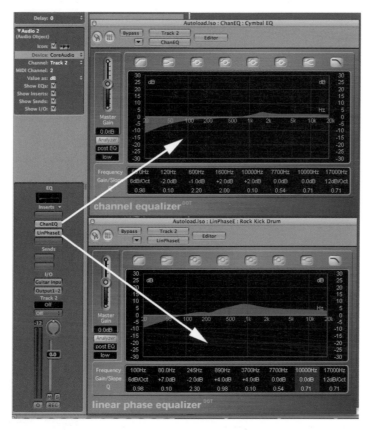

Figure 5.30
Channel EQ and Linear Phase EQ

The difference is in the name. The Linear Phase EQ preserves the phase of the EQ at all settings. In a normal EQ (such as the Channel EQ) phase changes as you change the settings. This isn't always a problem as these phase changes are part of the reason some EQs sound 'nicer' than others. The Linear Phase EQ could be said to sound 'neutral' whatever the setting – even at extreme EQ settings, it doesn't impart it's own character. The downside of the Linear Phase EQ is that it uses more CPU power than the humble Channel EQ.

- Use the Channel EQ for general EQ duties or when you want to impart its sound on a Track.
- Use the Linear Phase EQ when you want to EQ without changing the overall nature of the sound. This is particularly useful when mastering a mix.

Tip

The Linear Phase EQ and Channel EQ have an Analyzer button. When this is ON, a plot is displayed of the frequency spectrum of any audio passing through the EQ. You can choose the resolution of this plot – how smooth it is. The higher the resolution the slower the frequency plot will be updated. The Pre EQ/Post EQ toggle allows you to see the effect on the spectrum of the EQ. You can use this analyzer to compare the spectrum of a commercial CD and compare it to your mixes

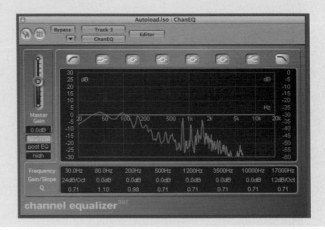

Match EQ

The Match EQ takes this comparison a stage further by actually allowing you to impose the frequency spectrum of an audio recording onto another. The idea is that you can take a recording you like the sound of and modify yours to suit using the Match EQ. Bear in mind that the Match EQ can't perform miracles – there's more to a sound that EQ. However, You may want to try the following;.

Figure 5.32
The Match EQ

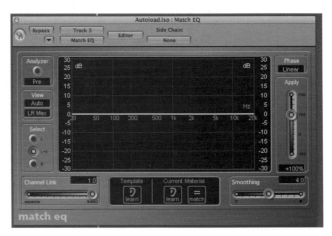

- Impose the EQ curve of a commercial song you like on one of your own.
- Impose the EQ curve of acoustic guitar recorded with a Microphone onto one recorded with a pickup – or even an electric guitar.
- Impose the EQ curve of a sitar on a guitar – or two completely different instruments for an unusual effect.

Here's how to use the match EQ.

- Instance the match EQ on a Track. The Region on the Track is the one we are trying to impose the EQ onto.
- Hold down the Control key and click (or right click) on the Template Learn box.
- Load in the source file – the audio file you want to use as your template EQ. This could be a commercial CD whose frequency spectrum you want to emulate. You'll see the spectrum of this file displayed.

Figure 5.33 (left)

Figure 5.34

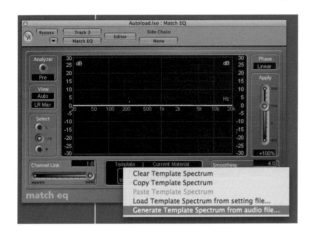

Click on the Current Material Match button. The EQ spectrum is imposed on the Track the match EQ is inserted on. You can use the Apply slider to change the intensity of the EQ change.

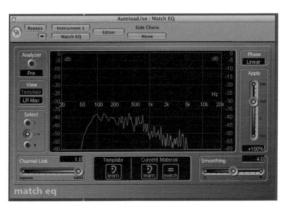

Figure 5.35

MultiPressor and the AUMultiband Compressor

These are both plug-ins that split the audio into several separate audio bands and each is then compressed separately. With a normal compressor, if you try to compress a signal with a prominent bass, say, that will have a disproportionate effect on the compression effect. This is particularly a problem when compressing whole mixes. So the idea with a Mult-band compressor is to split the signal into bass, mids and high frequencies and compress these separately thus minimizing these problems. They are particularly useful when mastering a stereo mix.

The AUMultiband Compressor

This is a simple (though nice sounding) multi-band compressor and, as it's pretty simple, it's easy to understand. It has four separate frequency bands.

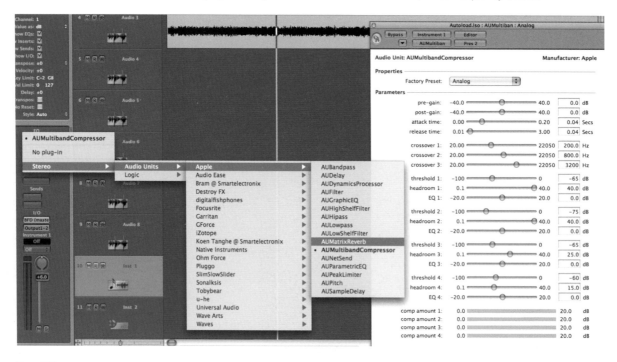

Figure 5.36
The AUMultiband Compressor

Here are the parameters you need to make it work.

Crossover

These three controls define the frequency ranges the bands will work over. A good starting point is the settings shown in the figure.

- The compressor in band 1 will compress the range 20Hz to 200Hz
- The compressor in band 2 will compress the range 200Hz to 800Hz
- The compressor in band 3 will compress the range 800Hz to 3200Hz
- The compressor in band 4 will compress the range 3200Hz to 220050Hz

Threshold

The Threshold controls act in the same way as on a single Channel Compressor. Bringing the Threshold level down increases the compression effect.

The headroom controls are used to make up the gain lost when you pull the threshold controls down.

Start by listening to the audio and try and gauge where the problems are. Do you need more consistency in the level of the mid range? Are the high frequencies too prominent? Look at the meters at the bottom of the window.

> **Info**
>
> As usual with EQ, you need to adjust parameters while using your ears. You can't 'see' an EQ!

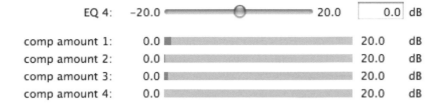

Figure 5.37

These will give you an idea of the overall balance. If you feel that one of the frequency ranges sounds wrong, try adjusting the Threshold and Headroom controls for that frequency. Remember: bringing down the Threshold increases the compression, evening out the sound and you'll probably need to increase the Headroom slider to compensate.

Figure 5.38

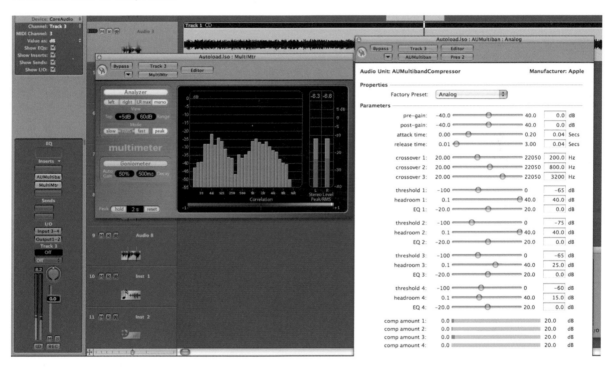

Attack Time

The Attack Time controls adjust how fast the compression happens – i.e. how long it takes to turn the level down. If this is set to a high value, transients will pass through before the compressor has time to react.

Release Time

The Release Time controls how fast the signal returns to its normal level. Setting too slow a release time will cause a 'pumping' effect – which can be a good thing in some circumstances.

Info

If you are using a Multiband compressor to master, try looking at the EQ curve of a song you like the sound of by inserting a Channel EQ and using the Analyzer (or the Multimeter) to see the EQ curve. You can then insert a Channel EQ on the master output after the Multi band compressor so you can see the effect the Multiband is having on the sound.

The MultiPressor

This is a more sophisticated Multiband compressor, but it works in the same way as the AUMultiBand compressor. You can set the Compression ratio, Attack, Release and Threshold separately for each band.

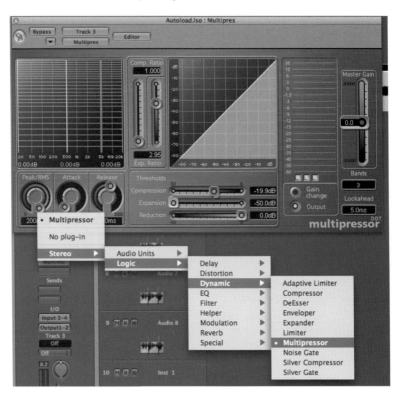

To use it you select the number of bands you wish to use (left). The frequency range over which each band works is chosen by dragging the sides of the bands. Select a band (below left). Adjust the controls for that band (below right), then select another band and repeat.

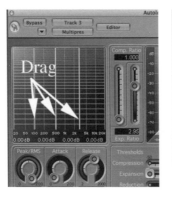

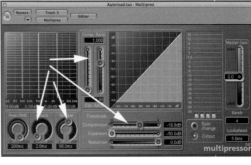

Workflow

This chapter has some tips that will allow you to speed up your workflow when using Logic – and make it more pleasing to the eye!

Customising how Logic looks

Not everyone likes the default look of Logic. There are a few ways to change the way things look.

The Display Preferences

The Display Preferences General window
- Anti aliased text. Turning this off can look better on some screens. It also speeds up screen redraws, which may be important on pre G5 Macs.
- Large local windows. If you are using high resolution or working at a distance, you can increase the size of the menus in the windows.
- Wide song position line. This can be easier to see on some screens, especially laptop or LCD screens.
- Show help tags. When you drag a Region or Note a small text box appears with positional information. It can be in the way in some cases, so you can turn it off here.
- Show default values. This show or hides the values displayed in the Region Parameter box

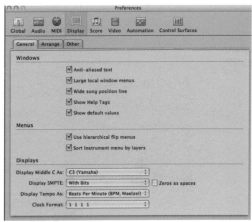

Figure 6.1

Figure 6.2

Figure 6.3

- Use Hierarchical Flip menus. When on, Logic menus have a right-pointing arrow which leads to other sub-menus.
- Sort Instrument menu by layers. When this is ON, the pull down menu on an Instrument object reflects the Layers in the Environment page. This makes it easy to keep track of Auxes used for multiple output Virtual instruments and other collections of similar objects.

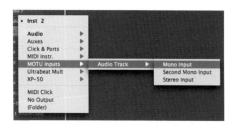

Figure 6.4

The Display Preferences Arrange window

- Muted regions are textured. When set to ON, it can be easier to locate muted Regions in a busy Arrange page.
- Background pattern. You can choose between the mausoleum-dark default Arrange page background or a more cheery light one.
- Plain background. If you select Plain Background from the Arrange page View menu, you can select a colour here. Again, this may make for a more pleasant appearance!

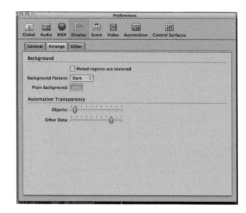

Figure 6.5

Figure 6.6

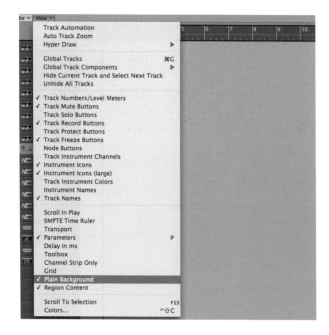

The Display Preferences Other window

- In this window you can change the appearance of the Matrix editor window.

Using colours

You can use colours to keep a track of various Regions in a Arrange page.

Setting a Track to a specific colour

Either choose a Track with no Regions on it or select the Track itself (and thus all Regions). From the Arrange page View menu, select Colors. A colour picker window opens and you can select a suitable colour.

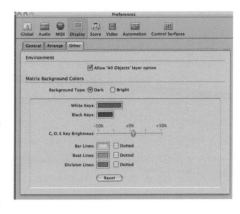

Figure 6.7

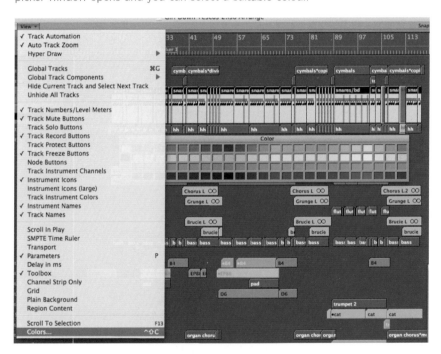

Figure 6.8

Any new Regions created on that Track will have the same colour.

Tip

If you have Tracks that are grouped together, say drums or backing vocals, you could make the Tracks which the Regions are playing on all the same colour.

Tip

You can colour most objects in Logic. You may want to colour similar Environment objects or all the hi-hat notes in the Matrix editor.

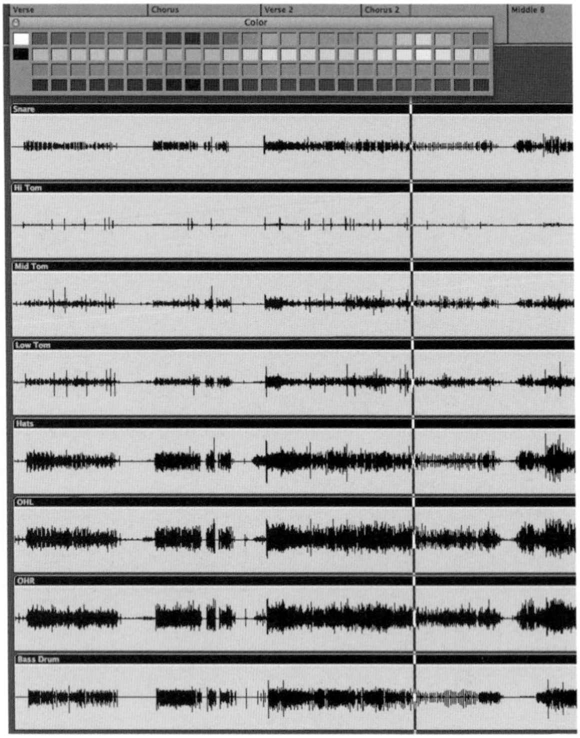

Figure 6.9

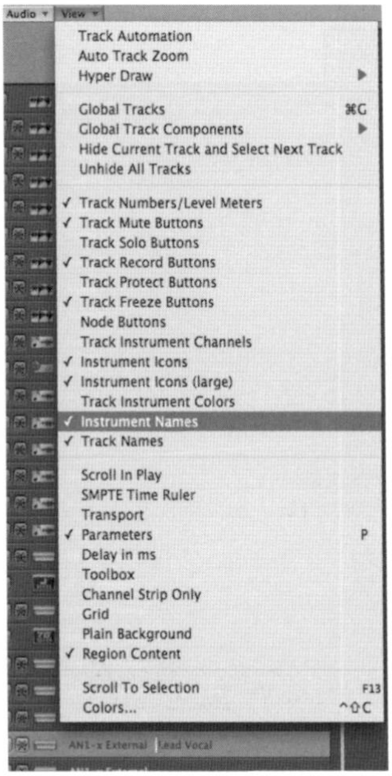

Figure 6.10

Figure 6.11

Instrument names in the Arrange page

If you select this function in the View menu, you can name Tracks.

This is really useful as these names then appear in the Track Mixer.

Figure 6.12

Tip

If you can't see the Instrument name box, drag the Track column to the right.

Using Icons

Each Object in Logic can have an Icon associated with it. If you select a Track in the Arrange page or an object in the Environment, you'll see the icon associated with it in the Track parameter box.

You can change the Icon by holding the mouse button on it. A list opens.

Figure 6.13

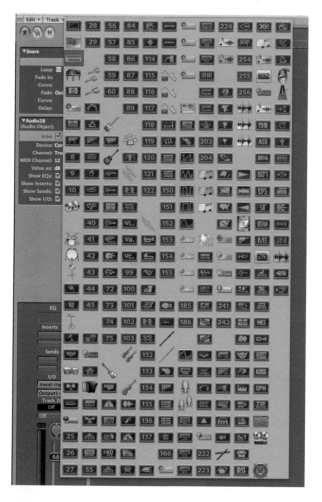

Figure 6.14

Choosing a suitable Icon can make finding Tracks in a busy Arrange page easier.

Info

You can use custom Icons in Logic. They are stored in the /Library/Application Support/Logic/Images/Icons folder. This folder isn't created by default. The Icon filenames should be xxx.png, where xxx is a 1 to 3 digit number. The Icons are 128x128 in sixe, must have an Alpha Channel for transparency and be saved in the Portable Graphics Format (.png) which most graphics software can export.

Tip

You should choose an icon filename of 326.png or above. Numbers 1-325.png are reserved for Logic's default Icons.

Transport

The Transport in Logic is particularly flexible. You can change its size and shape and have only portions of the Transport available. As you can have as many Transports open as you want you can completely customize your look.

Figure 6.15

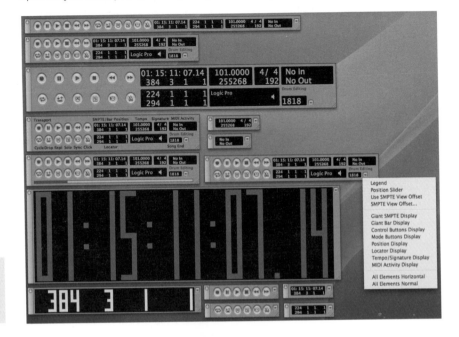

Info

You can insert a Transport at the top of the Arrange page from the page's View menu. Clicking and holding on the Transport buttons brings up various menus related to Transport functions.

Scroll in play

Normally, Logic moves the SPL as a Song plays. However, you can change this behavior. If you select Scroll in Play from the Arrange page View menu, the SPL will now remain static at the centre of the screen and the Regions will scroll by. You turn it on from the Arrange page View menu.

Zooming in Logic

Although you can set up different Screensets in Logic with different Zoom levels, many people prefer to work in a single window. You can use the Zoom controls at the top and bottom of a window.

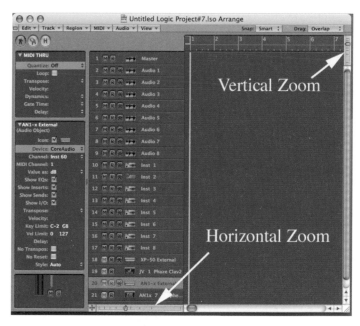

Figure 6.16

Or the mouse (as detailed in Chapter 3), but sometimes this is inconvenient and time consuming – and the mouse may not be at hand. Logic has several automatic zoom and Key Command functions related to Zoom.

Automatic track zooming

You can switch this on from the Arrange page View menu. Then, when you select a Track it is zoomed out with respect to all other Tracks.

Zooming individual Tracks

If you move the mouse to the bottom left of a Track, the cursor changes to a finger. You can then zoom each Track individually.

Figure 6.17 (left)

Figure 6.18

Zoom Key Commands

Figure 6.19

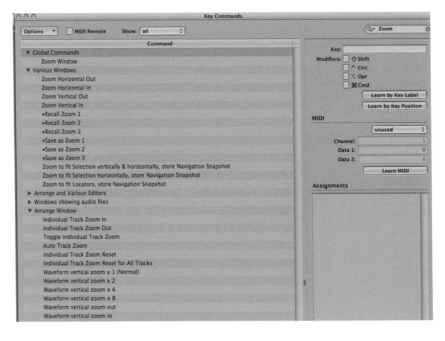

Using the zoom Key Commands is a handy way of changing the layout of a Logic screen. You may want to enlarge a Track so you can see where a waveform or MIDI data starts or ends or to check the lining up of Regions, then zoom back out to see an overview. The 'Recall Zoom' and 'Save as Zoom' Key Commands are particularly useful here for this.

Figure 6.20

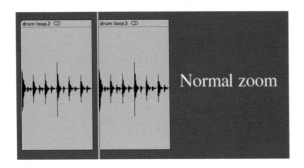

Figure 6.21

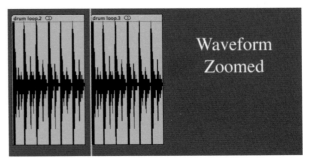

Zoom navigation history

Logic stores the last 30 zoom and scroll positions of open windows. You can navigate backwards and forwards though this navigation history using the Navigation: Back and Navigation: Forward Key Commands.

Opening windows

If you hold down the Option key when opening a Window from a menu item, the Window will always be 'On Top' on the screen. The narrow bar shows a window has been opened in this way.

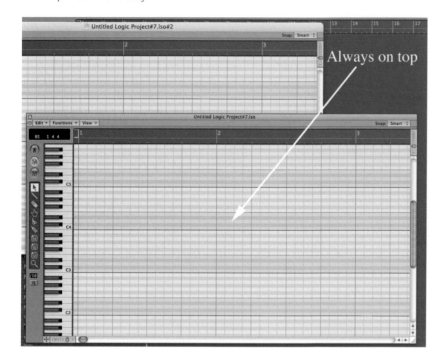

Figure 6.22

Figure 6.23

Process buffers

These somewhat mysterious buffers are located in the Audio Preferences Core Audio Drivers window. It's worth experimenting with this value. It usually defaults to Medium.

- A small Process Buffer can improve the responsiveness of Logic. It does however require more processing power – so you may get dropouts or other processing errors.
- A small Process Buffer reduces the amount of processing power required to run Logic. However, it will increase latency and may make Logic feel less responsive.

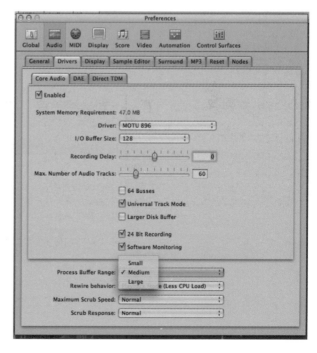

SMPTE Time ruler

The default ruler at the top of the Arrange and Editor pages is in Bars. You can add a SMPTE absolute time display using the Pages View menu. You may want to do this if you're working to picture.

You can choose the format of the display from the Display Preferences General window (Figure 6.25).

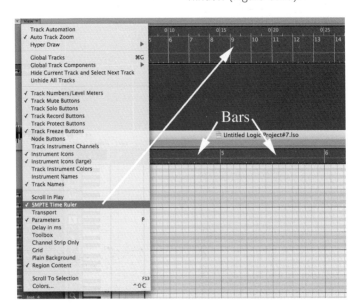

Figure 6.24

Figure 6.25

Using markers to display lyrics

You can use Logic as a kind of 'teleprompter' and display lyrics as it plays by using Markers.

First set up some Markers. You need one Marker per lyric section. For example, you may want to display each couplet as it comes along.

- Create some Markers at the position in the Song you want the lyric to change.

Tip

Use the Create Marker Key Command to easily create markers at the SPL.

Figure 6.26

Figure 6.28

- Open the Marker list window (Figure 6.27 right).
- Double click on a Marker and a text editor opens. Type in the lyric. Choose the Font and size (Figure 6.28).
- Close the text editor using the book icon (left). Double click on the next marker and repeat the process.

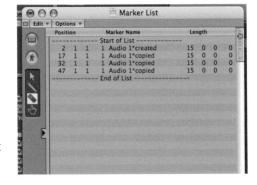

Once all the lyrics are input, close the marker list window. Now select the Options>marker>Open Text as float menu item. This opens the text editor so it's always on top. Align and resize as necessary. Make sure the Running Man icon is ON so the text editor changes as the Song progresses.

Now as you play the song, the text in the window will change at the required point.

Figure 6.29

Figure 6.30

Exporting Tracks and Regions as Audio files

You may want to convert whole tracks of audio or Virtual instruments, or Regions on a track to audio files for re-importing into Logic or for sending off to a colleague who is using another DAW. Use the File>Export menu to do this. This method of exporting saves files with all the automation and plug-in processing. It's like freezing, but you can choose which file format to use.

You can then drag the exported files back into Logic.

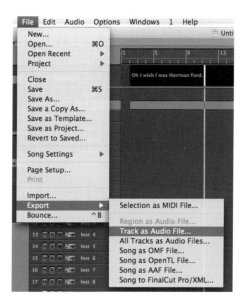

Figure 6.31

> **Tip**
>
> This technique is really useful if you wish to collaborate with someone who doesn't use Logic – perhaps they are using Pro Tools or Cubase? If you export all the Tracks, all your collaborator has to do is to load in all the audio files and line them up at the start.

> **Tip**
>
> If you want to archive a recording (incase your DAW or plug-ins are not available in the future) or your collaborator wishes to get the audio 'raw', that is without being processed by plug-ins, you'll have to bypass all of the plug-ins and disable automation and set all the Pan and Volume controls to '0' (Option-click on a control to do this). Don't forget to do this with any Auxes and Busses too.

> **Tip**
>
> Make sure you export the files in the format your collaborator can use.

Environment tips

Layers

Logic's Environment can seem complicated and can contain a lot of objects all cabled together. It makes sense to keep related objects on separate pages or Layers. You could, for example, have a Layer containing an editor for a synthesizer, another for

Audio objects, or another for the Auxes that a multiple output virtual Instrument is cabled to.

Figure 6.32

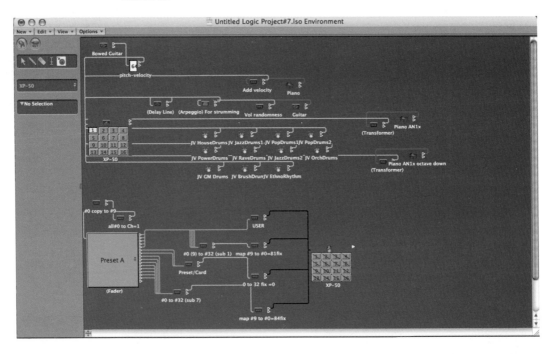

Layers are created by clicking and holding on the Layer box. You can also select Layers here.

Layers are named by double clicking on the Layer name.

Layers appear in the pull-down menus in the Arrange page Instrument Tracks.

Figure 6.34

Figure 6.33

Figure 6.35

Environment objects

The Environment contains many useful objects that are used to modify the flow of MIDI data. You can use these with external MIDI equipment or Virtual Instruments.

Figure 6.36

Using the Arpeggiator

Logic has a rather nifty Arpeggiator. Here's how you set it up and use it.

Open the Environment and create a new Page. Call it Arpeggiators. Create an Arpeggiator object from the Environment page New menu. Hold down the Option key and click on the little arrow on the Arpeggiator object. You can now cable the Arpeggiator to the required sound source. In this example, it's cabled to Instrument object 1 which has an ES1 loaded info on it. Hold down the Option key and click on the little arrow at the top right of the Arpeggiator.

Select the Arpeggiator object. You'll see in the Parameter box the different parameters that can be used with the Arpeggiator. Make sure the box next to the icon is ticked. Rename it to something useful and give it a nice icon.

To use the Arpeggiator, select it in the Arrange page and put Logic into play. The Arpeggiator only works when Logic is running. Play some notes and chords to hear the effect and change Arpeggiator parameters to hear their effect. Then use the 'Capture last take' Key Command to record the results.

Figure 6.37

Figure 6.38

Figure 6.39

The Transformer

Using controller pedals in Logic

A lot of software these days, especially orchestral plug-ins, make use of MIDI controller data in an attempt to improve the realism of a performance. They may for example, use the Expression MIDI control change message (cc11) to adjust vital aspects of volume and timbre. If you are using an expression pedal into a master keyboard you can often set-up the keyboard to determine which MIDI control number is output into Logic when you move the pedal. However, when you are running several different plug-ins with different MIDI controller number requirements it can become inconvenient to keep reselecting the correct one on the master keyboard. You can use Logic's Environment to make this easier to manage.

Open the Environment and create a new layer. Create two Monitors, an Instrument and Transformer object. Cable and rename them as shown in Figure 6.41.

If you then Option/Click on the little arrow on the

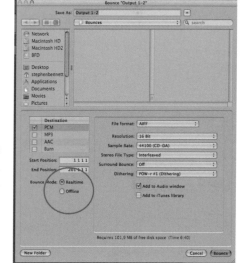

Figure 3.40

Figure 6.41

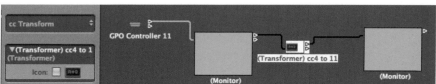

second Monitor object, you can cable this to your plug-in – in this case, the GPO, which is inserted on Audio Instrument 2. Double click on the Transformer object and enter the parameters as in Figure 6.43.

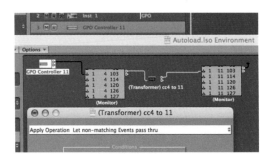

Figure 6.43

Figure 6.42

If you now select the Instrument ('GPO Controller 11') in the Arrange page and move the foot pedal, the required MIDI cc will be sent to GPO. As you can see from the last figure, the transformer is converting MIDI cc 4 to MIDI cc 11.

Using Multi-timbral external hardware synthesisers in Logic

You'll need to use the Environment to create a Multi Instrument object that you can use with the external Mutli Timbral synthesizer.

From the New menu, create a multi-instrument and drag it to the top left of the Environment window. Make sure there is not a tick in the box next to Icon in the Parameter box for this object.

Rename the object to the real name of your MIDI device by highlighting it and double clicking on the name in the Parameter box – 'Multi Instr.'.

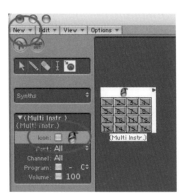

Figure 6.44

Figure 6.45

Now select the port the MIDI device is connected to using the pull down menu on the Parameter list (Figure 6,46).

Click on the '1' on the Multi instrument so it is uncrossed and highlighted. This selects the sub-instrument that will use MIDI channel 1 on your synthesiser. Click on the box next to Program, so the instrument will receive program changes. Make sure the box next to Icon is crossed too so you can select it in the Arrange page. Notice that the Parameter box changes as well. It now displays the Parameters for the sub-channel rather than the whole multi-instrument object.

Now open an Arrange page. You can select the Roland XP50 MIDI channel '1' from the pull down menu in the Track Column. Notice that the Environment layers are shown here too. Select 'Roland XP 1 Grand Piano' from the 'Synths' layer. Play a note on your MIDI keyboard. You should hear sound out of your synthesiser. It probably won't be Grand Piano sound though!

Figure 6.46 (above)

Figure 6.47

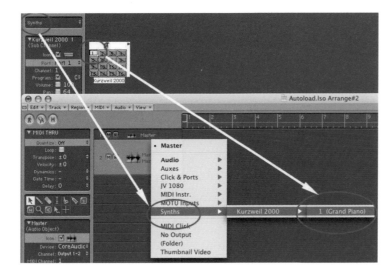

Figure 6.48

If you don't hear a sound, check the following:

- Make sure all your MIDI cables are connected correctly and your synthesizer is connected to an amplifier or headphones. Check the Audio Midi Setup application from the Applications/Utilities folder and check that your MIDI interface is connected.
- When you press your MIDI keyboard, do you see values appearing in the IN and OUT boxes on the transport bar?
- If there are no IN values, check the connections between the MIDI OUT and MIDI IN on your computer. If there are no OUT values make sure you have set the correct port in the Multi-instrument and the MIDI cables.

Figure 6.49

Figure 6.50

To set up the next channel, click on the '2' on the Multi instrument so it is uncrossed and highlighted.

Click on the box next to Program, so the instrument will receive program changes. Make sure the box next to Icon is crossed too.

Repeat this for all 16 MIDI channels if you require them. The pull-down menu on the Arrange page should now look something like Figure 6.51.

Figure 6.51

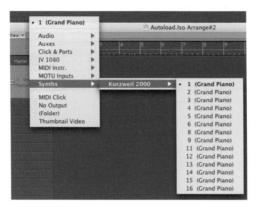

Of course all the sounds on the Roland XP50 aren't Grand Pianos! Fortunately, Logic provides a way to name all the patches that actually are loaded into your synthesiser. You can then select these by name, rather than just a choosing a patch number. Double click on the top of the Multi Instrument. This will open a patch name box.

Of course these default names are unlikely to be the ones on your synthesiser, so

Figure 6.52

Figure 6.53

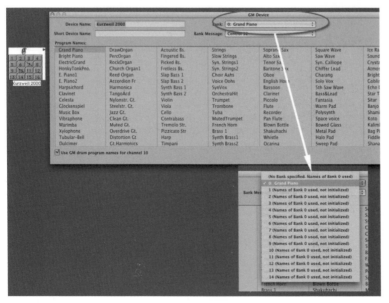

you'll have to rename them appropriately.

Select bank 0 from the pull down menu. Your synthesiser may need special bank change parameters. You'll need to look in the manual of your MIDI device, and select the appropriate Bank Message from the menu.

Now delete all the names in the window by choosing 'Cut all names' from the pull down menu (Figure 6.54).

Now you can type in the names of the patches on your synthesiser (Figure 6.55). Double click on each of the boxes in turn and type in the correct name of the patch. When you have finished typing in all the names in a bank, change to the next bank. Logic will initialize it for you, and then you can continue to enter patch names.

Figure 6.54

As you can imagine, it can take quite a while to type in patch names on a synthesiser that has 16 banks of 128 sounds! Luckily you can copy the patch names from either a patch editor or another Logic song that has the names of the patches for your synthesisers already entered.

Figure 6.55

You can find a lot of Logic songs containing this sort of thing on the Internet. See http://www.pc-publishing.com/logiclinks.

Song information

This feature can be found in the main Options menu. It gives various useful information about your Song.

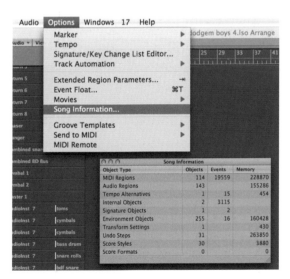

Figure 6.56

Figure 6.57

MIDI Reset

If you get hung MIDI notes, you can reset the MIDI interface by double-clicking on the Input/Output section of the Transport.

The Arrange page, Editor windows and sundry editing tips

General editing tips

Working with Regions

Holding the Option key while cutting a Region with the Scissors tool will split it into equal slices.

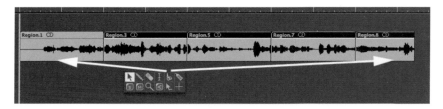

Figure 7.1

If you drag the mouse over an audio (or MIDI) Region, you'll be able to listen for the points you want to edit (scrubbing).

Removing Overlaps

When you record MIDI data in real time it's likely you'll get notes overlapping.

These notes can cause prob-

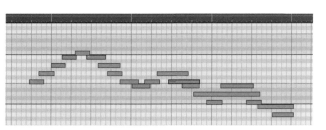

Figure 7.2

lems with Drum plug-ins and monophonic lines. You can get rid of these overlaps in the Matrix and List editors by selecting the notes and using the Functions>Note Events overlap correction menu items.

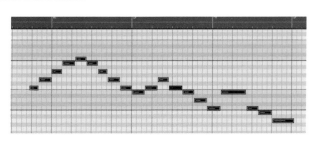

Figure 7.3

Removing Duplicates

In a similar fashion, any doubles notes can be removed using the Editor's Function>Erase MIDI events>Duplicates menu item.

Inputs and outputs

In certain editors, the following icons are available. They deal with the input and output of MIDI data.

  When on, allows MIDI data to be input via an external MIDI device.

  When on, clicking on an event outputs it to your MIDI devices.

Figure 7.4   **Figure 7.5**

Default editor window

You can set which editor window opens when you double-click on a MIDI Region from the Global Preferences Editing window.

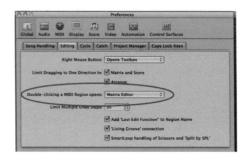

Figure 7.6

The Sample editor will always open when you double-click on an Audio Region

Selecting events in the Editors

Alongside the selection criteria in a window's Edit menu, some editors have Function menus that have select options in their Note Events menu. This is from the Matrix editor.

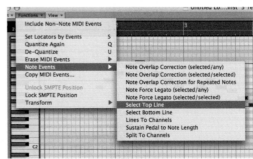

- Selecting Top Line is useful for extracting the melody line from a chordal keyboard part.
- Selecting Bottom Line is useful for extracting the bass line from a chordal keyboard part.

Figure 7.7

Using Key Commands in the Arrange page and Editors.

There are several Key Commands associated with each editor, which can help in selecting and moving around.

- Select First/last/Previous and Next Event. These Key Commands allow you to quickly navigate the Regions in the Arrange page and notes and other MIDI data in the other Editors.
- Select inside Locators and Deselect outside Locators. These commands make it easy to delete and copy whole sections of a Song.
- Select Muted Regions. This Key Command is used to select (then remove if you wish) muted Regions you may not be using in a Song.
- Select First/last/Previous and Next Track. Use these Key Commands in the Arrange page to help move around the screen using the computer keyboard.
- Select First/last/Previous and Next Region. Use these Key Commands in the Arrange page to help move around the screen using the computer keyboard.

Hyperdraw in the Arrange page and the Editing windows

Hyperdraw is Logic's older Region based automation system. For more general automation, you'll probably want to use Logics more accurate Track-based system. But it's still useful for these reasons.

- It can be used to draw MIDI controller curves
- It can be used for fine editing of volume and controllers on a per-region basis.

Hyperdraw is a way of drawing controller information directly on the Regions themselves. You can draw any controller information but the most useful are obviously volume, pan, modulation, aftertouch and pitchbend.

Open the Matrix or Score Editors. Make the Hyperdraw area visible from the View Hyperdraw menu.

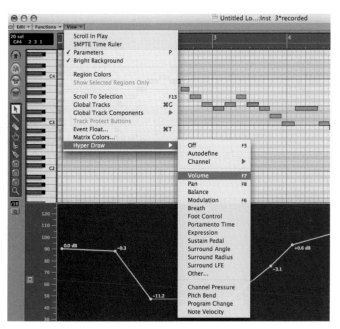

Figure 7.8

Figure 7.9 (right)

Figure 7.10

Tip

Holding down the Ctrl key while dragging makes the movement finer. You will only be able to move vertically though.

Choosing a Hyprdraw controller

Either select a controller from the View>Hyperdraw menu. Or click on the small arrow at the left of the Hyperdraw window and choose a controller from there.

For this example, choose controller 7 (Volume).

Now click on the Region to draw a Hyperdraw curve. At each click, a MIDI Volume (controller number 7) event (node) is created and a line drawn between them. Events can be dragged and moved at will.

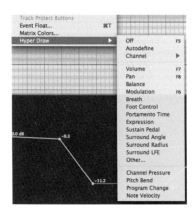

Moving the whole curve

Holding down the Option while you drag a Hyperdraw event, moves all the Hyperdraw nodes to the right of the node you click on.

Deleting individual Hyperdraw events

Click on each event to delete it. The line is re-drawn between the nearest two events.

Deleting all the Hyperdraw events

Hold down the Option key and double click on a node to delete all the events.

Figure 7.11

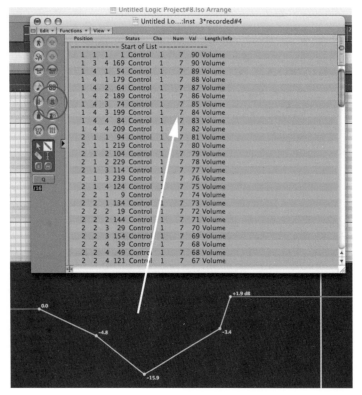

Finer editing of Hyperdraw events

Highlight the region. Open the Event List editor. Make sure just the controller data icon is on and the Note icon is OFF. This will ensure only controller events are displayed. You can see and edit all the nodes you have just created.

If you want to draw the curve for a different controller number, let's say Pan (controller number 10), select it from the View>Hyperdraw>menu item. The volume data curve on the region is greyed out. You can now draw on the Region in the same fashion as for the volume curve.

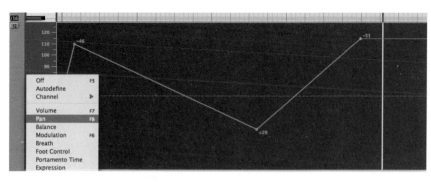

Figure 7.12

Hyperdraw can be useful with Virtual instruments that use unusual controllers. Some orchestral libraries use multiple controllers to help produce a realistic result – they may control timbre, volume, vibtaro, bow strokes and so on.

Tip

You can bring to the front and re-edit the previous Volume Hyperdraw events by choosing the View>Hyperdraw>Volume menu item.

The Hyper editor

Using the Hyper editor as a drum editor
Logic does not have a dedicated drum editor. As it is sometimes useful when editing drum parts to see the notes on a grid, you can use the Hyper editor to perform this function.

The easiest way to set up a hyperset as a drum editor is as to create a mapped instrument of your drum and percussion sounds.

How to set up a Mapped instrument
In the Environment window select the New>Mapped Instrument menu item. A window will open. Close it. Move the Mapped instrument to a convenient place.

Figure 7.13

In our example, the Mapped instrument would control an Alesis D4 drum module, but it could just as easily be any Virtual instrument, drum machine or sound on a Multi timbral synth.

Highlight the mapped instrument and change the MIDI channel to 10 in the Cha field in the Parameter box. While it's Highlighted, rename it, make sure there is a cross in the box next to the Icon in the Parameter box and make sure you can see the cables from the View>Cables menu item. Set the Port: to OFF – this mapped instrument will only be used to control the Alesis D4 drum module.

Figure 7.14

Cable the Mapped instrument to the Alesis D4 Multi by dragging the cable from the little arrow at the top right. If the Instrument object is on another Environment page, hold down the Option key when you click and choose it from the pull down menu. Remove the channel port setting when asked by Logic.

Rename the Mapped instrument to something useful – 'Alesis D4Mapped Instrument'

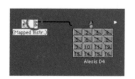

Figure 7.15

Figure 7.16

Figure 7.17

If you look in the instrument menu on the track column in the Arrange page you will see the Mapped instrument. Select it and check it plays your drum sounds.

If you want the Mapped instrument to play a Virtual plug-in (such as Ultrabeat or the EXS24 sampler, cable the Mapped instrument to the Audio object the Virtual instrument is on. Remove the channel port setting when asked by Logic.

Figure 7.17a

Figure 7.18

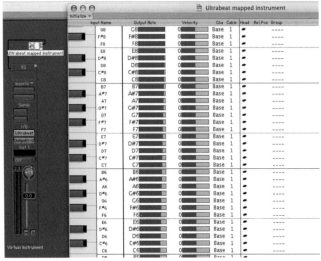

We'll use this connection to create the Mapped instrument.

Double click on the Mapped instrument to open the window again.

The window has the following properties:

• Click on the keyboard to the left of the window; it will play the sounds assigned to that key.

• Double click on the name of a drum sound to change it.

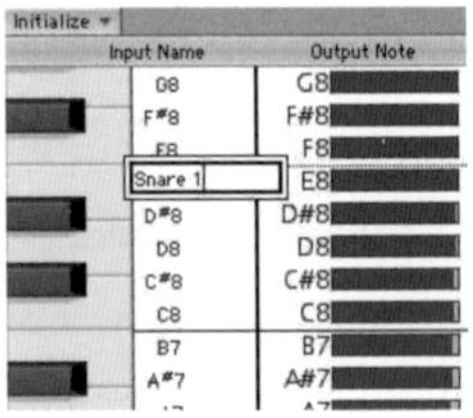

Figure 7.19

You can then give each drum (or key) its own name.

- Open the Hyperedit window. Record a short sequence using all the sounds assigned to keys. Just click on the pause and record button on the transport bar (or select record via a key command) and play each note in turn. No need to press play. Then stop recording. Remember; don't press play!
- Make sure the sequence is selected and then open the Hyper editor.
- Select HYPER>CREATE HYPER SET menu item. Double click on 'set initialized' and enter a useful name, Like 'Ultrabeat drums 1'
- Click on the volume event definition and select the HYPER>DELETE EVENT DEFINITION menu item.
- Select the HYPER>MULTI CREATE EVENT DEFINITION menu item. In the Dialog box which appears, select ALL (all events in current sequence). You will see something like Figure 7.20.

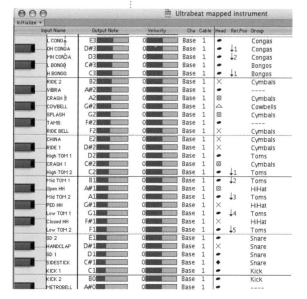

Figure 7.20

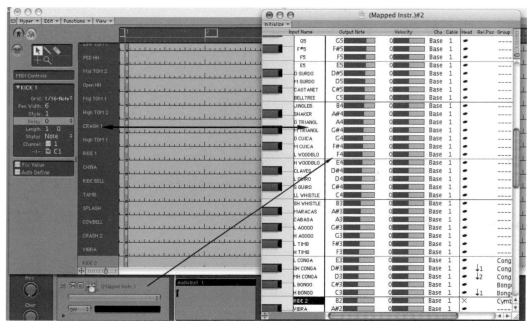

The names of the drums down the left of the window are imported from your Mapped instrument.

Figure 7.21

- Select the EDIT>SELECT ALL menu item.
- Press the delete key to delete the drum events, i.e. the notes you played in.
- Adjust the zoom of the window as desired.

You can now enter drum data directly with the pencil tool or by recording as usual from the MIDI keyboard (you may want to switch the File>Song settings>Recording>Merge new recordings with selected regions menu item to ON, if you want to loop around and add new notes at each pass. Step time input is also useful when writing drum parts.

You can delete notes with the eraser tool and drag them around as with any events in Logic. You can also change the grid values for each event definition.

If you want to adjust the grid value of several event definitions, just Shift click on them to select them all. Grid values are changed in the Parameter box.

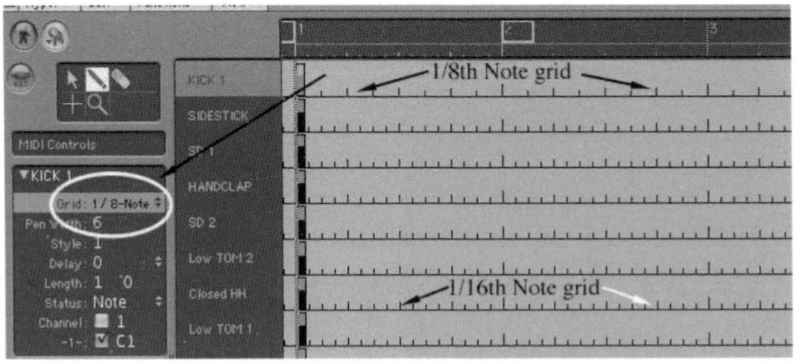

Figure 7.22

You may want the bass drum (Kick 1) to default to $1/8^{th}$ note, the Open HH to 1/16, so select these individually and edit the Grid parameter.

Tip

The Grid value defines where new notes will appear on the Hyper edit window when you create them with the pencil tool. It's a sort of pre-quantize effect. For example, if you want to add a bass drum on every bar, change the grid value to 1:1. You can then only pencil in notes on the first beat of the bar. If you want to create hi-hats on every 16th beat, set the grid value to 1/16. Now, dragging the pencil across the Hyper editor, will create a hi-hat note on every 16th beat. You can, of course, change the grid value after you have drawn events. Grid values are changed in the Parameter box.

The velocities of the notes are shown as the dark areas of the note columns. These can be edited with the pencil tool. Note how easy it is to draw a variable velocity on the 'Tite HH' in Figure 7.23.

Figure 7.23

Speaking of Hi Hats, next to the Hi Hats in the 'Drum Editor' in the next figure are some little dots with lines through them. These mean that these channel definitions are in 'Hi Hat mode' (just click to the left of the name to switch it on or off). What this means is that only one event can be output at the same time when in this mode. You may want this to happen if you are trying to emulate a human drummer more closely – only closed or open hi-hats can be played on one set at a time.

Figure 7.24

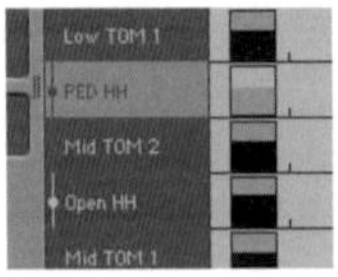

Of course, you can group any instruments like this. You may want a monophonic bass line for example. The Hyper editor isn't just for drum notes!

Time stretching and tempo adjustment in the Arrange page

When you record MIDI data you can change the tempo of a song at will. However, any audio files (that are not Apple loops or newly recorded into Logic 7.1 or later) will not change tempo. What you need is some way of stretching an audio region to fit the new Tempo. Luckily, Logic can do this.

Here's the original recording of audio and MIDI at the original tempo of 120bpm.

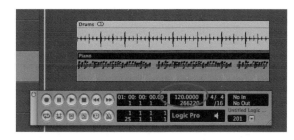

Figure 7.25

If you change the tempo to 130bpm, the MIDI data changes along with Logic, but the audio doesn't. You can change the tempo of the audio file from the two options in the Arrange page Audio menu (Figure 7.28).

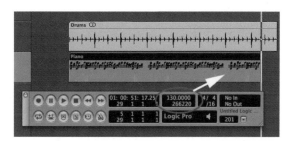

Figure 7.26

If you are using Logic 7 or later, any audio recorded into Logic can automatically follow the tempo changes in a Song. You turn this feature on and off using the Track parameter box Follow Tempo: function.

Figure 7.27

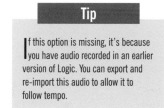

Tip

If this option is missing, it's because you have audio recorded in an earlier version of Logic. You can export and re-import this audio to allow it to follow tempo.

Adjust Region length to Locators

To use this feature, first set the locators to the bar length you require. In this case, you could select the MIDI file and use the 'Set Locators by Region' Key Command to set the locators.

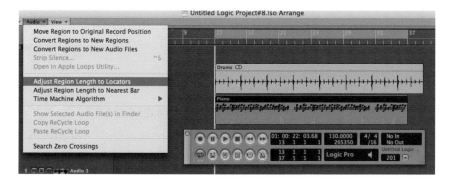

Figure 7.28

Now select the audio Region and choose the Arrange page>Audio >Adjust Region length to Locators menu item, to fit the audio to the tempo.

Figure 7.29

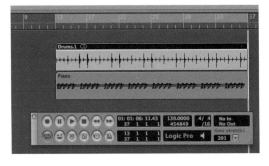

Adjust Region length to nearest bar

This is similar to the Adjust Region length feature, but adjusts the audio Region tempo to the nearest bar. In this case the result would be identical.

The quality of the time stretching is defined by the algorithm you set in the Arrange page>Audio>Time Machine Algorithm menu.

Figure 7.30

Time Machine Algorithms

The top 6 options in this menu are always available. Choose the one that best suits your audio recording.

The bottom 3 options are installed as part of the OSX 10.4 or later Operating System. They are superior to the top 6 algorithms. You should try these first if you have the option.

Arrange page tips

Adding audio files

You can add audio regions directly to the Arrange window in various ways. You need to select an Audio track for these to work.

• Hold down the shift key and click with the Pencil tool. That brings up the standard audio dialogue for opening files. The selected file will be added to the

Audio window, and a Region will be placed at the mouse cursor on the Arrange page
- Drag audio files from the Finder onto the Arrange page directly. If you drag multiple files, they will be placed on consecutive tracks.
- Use the 'Import audio' Key Command.

Matrix editor tips

Figure 7.31

The Event Float
The Event float is a small editor window that displays information about any selected note or Region. You can open it from the Options menu, but it makes more sense to assign it to the 'Open Event float' Key Command.

Hyperdraw
You can use Hyperdraw in the Matrix editor. It's selected from the View menu item.

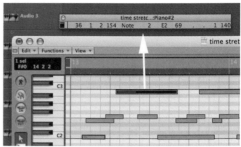

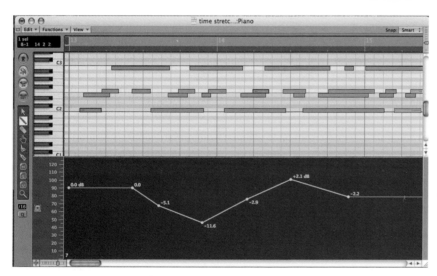

Figure 7.32

Event List editor tips

Viewing events
Select which data is displayed from the icons in the editor.

- View, edit and add note data.
- View, edit and add program changes.
- View, edit and add Pitchbend data.
- View, edit and add Controller data.
- View, edit and add channel pressure – channel aftertouch.
- View, edit and add polyphonic pressure – polyphonic aftertouch.
- View, edit and add Systems exclusive data.
- View, edit and add Meta events.

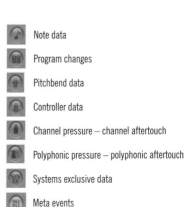

Note data

Program changes

Pitchbend data

Controller data

Channel pressure – channel aftertouch

Polyphonic pressure – polyphonic aftertouch

Systems exclusive data

Meta events

Score editor tips

Just because a Song sounds good on playback, doesn't mean it will produce a playable score. Here's some tips that can help out. You'll probably want to do this in the Matrix editor.

Remove overlaps

If you have overlaps they can cause confusion in a score. Remove them by selecting all the notes in a Region and using the Matrix editor Functions>Note Events>Note event correction.

Remove doubles

In a similar fashion, you can remove any duplicate notes using the Functions>Erase MIDI events> Duplicates menu item.

Quantize

Use Logic's quantize menu to improve the appearance and playability of the score.

Figure 7.33

Figure 7.34

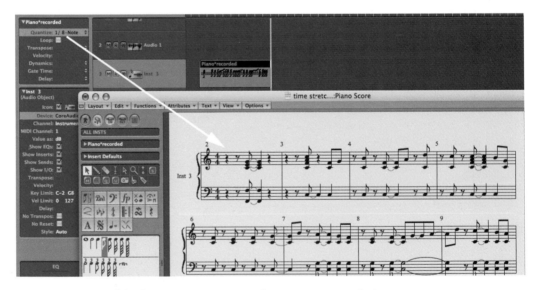

Other Parameters you can use to improve your score output

Score Styles

As you can see, from the previous figure Logic has automatically picked up the fact a Piano was recorded and has split the stave into bass and treble. What has in fact happened, is that Logic has chosen the default

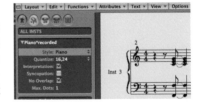

Figure 7.35

Score style 'Piano' in the display Parameter box.

If you hold and click on the Style Parameter, you can get a list of all the predefined score styles. Change them and see how they affect the score display.

If you want to edit a score style, double click on it in the display Parameter box; a window will open.

Here you can change the parameters of the score style. In most cases, the

Figure 7.36

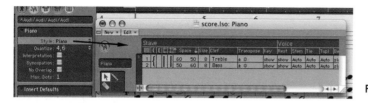

Figure 7.37

defaults can be left as they are, but all the parameters in the window can be edited with the mouse. You may want to change

- the SPACE between staves
- the TRP or transpose values of the staves
- the SPLIT point of the staves

Display Quantization

As well as quantizing the actual MIDI data in the Matrix Editor, you can quantize the DISPLAY of the notes in the Score Editor. The Default quantization is based on the display format from the Transport bar.

There is a pop up menu displayed when you click and hold down the mouse key over the Quantize field.

There are a collection of quantization (such as 4, 8 etc.) values and hybrid (4,3 etc.) values. The hybrid and higher resolution values work best where the original part is played with accuracy.

Interpretation

One of the most powerful features in Logic is its ability to suppress rests that may occur if a note is stopped short or played a little after the beat. This is toggled ON and OFF from the Interpretation parameter in the display Parameter box.

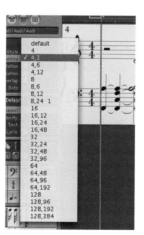

Info

This quantize ONLY affects what you see, not what you hear.

Figure 7.38

Tip

Get it right before you score! You'll find it less frustrating and less time consuming if you play accurately, quantize and correct overlaps BEFORE you open the score editor.

Figure 7.39

Here's a piano part with Interpretation set to OFF.

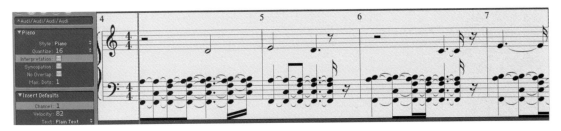

Figure 7.40

Here's the piano part with Interpretation set to ON.

Syncopation

When it is ON, the notes are displayed as actual note values.

Figure 7.41

When this parameter is OFF syncopations are displayed as smaller note values tied across the beat.

Figure 7.42

No Overlap

When this is on, it suppresses the display of portions of notes, which overlap past the beginning of new notes.

This is overlap OFF. Note all the spurious ties.

Figure 7.43

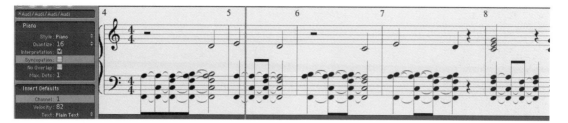

This is overlap set to ON. You can normally leave this ON.

Figure 7.44

Maximum Dots

This sets the maximum number of dots that can be displayed after a note. The setting you choose depends on what you want your score to look like. If you don't know what to put in here, leave it set to 1.

> **Tip**
>
> All these parameters affect the DISPLAY only, so experiment with their settings and values. You can't damage anything!

Audio window and the Sample editor tips

Sample-accurate editing

Although most editing of audio files can be performed in the Arrange page, the fine editing is not sample accurate – i.e. you cannot fine-tune the start and end point of an audio file at sample level resolution. However, you can do this in the Sample editor.

Double click on the Region to open it in the Sample editor.

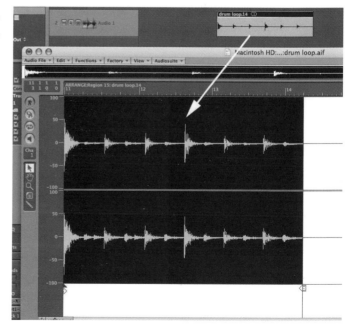

Figure 7.45

You can change the Region start point by dragging the S flag. The Anchor point (the actual start of the audio in the Region) will also move. You can change the Region end point by dragging the E flag.

Figure 7.46

Figure 7.47

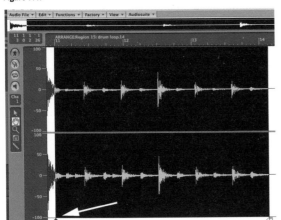

The Anchor point is the actual start of the Audio – it can be in a different place from the Region start and will move the audio in the Arrange page.

Other useful stuff in the Sample editor

Use the Sample editor to destructively fade, silence and trim audio files.

Use the Remove DC Offset function if you have 'thumps' in your audio.

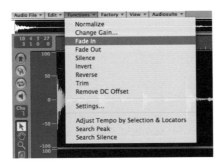

Use the Search Silence function to find gaps in long audio files. Use the Search Peak function to detect clipping in an audio file. It will pick up any peak that reaches 0dB.

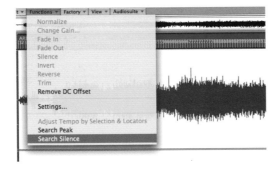
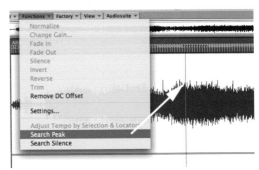

Apple loops and fluid audio

Apple loops are specialized audio files that can easily be tempo matched to a song. Apple loops can also contain information about their content, making them searchable. Logic ships with many Apple loops and you can make your own using the supplied Apple loop utility. It's easier to see how Apple loops fit into the scheme of things within Logic by using an example.

Open the Loops browser from the Audio>Loop browser menu item.

Figure 8.1

If you have any Apple loops installed in the default location, /Library/Application Support/GarageBand, you'll see them displayed here.

To audition an Apple loop click on it.

To add an Apple loop to a song, drag it to the Arrange page from the Loop browser.

Tip

You can store Apple loops anywhere you like and load them into Logic by dragging them from the Finder to the Arrange page or using the Audio>Import audio file menu item. But if you want them to appear in the browser you'll need to place them in /Library/Application Support/GarageBand folder.

Figure 8.2

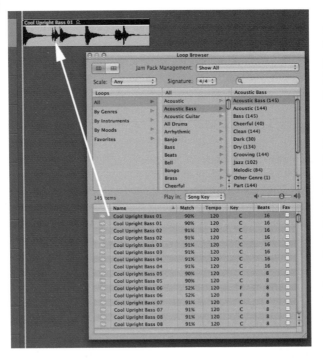

Now change the tempo in Logic. You'll hear that the audio in the Apple loops changes tempo too.

Apple loops have Tags associated with them. These tags provide information about the audio in the Apple loop, so you can use the search window in the browser and the scale and signature information to find the loops you need. You can see, create and modify this information in the Apple loops utility.

Figure 8.3

The Apple Loop Utility

This is a separate program stored in the Applications folder – though you can also load it from the Arrange page>Audio>Open in Apple loops. When you do this, Logic asks you to enter the loop length in bars or beats.

The following figure has the drum Apple Loop shown above, loaded.

Figure 8.4

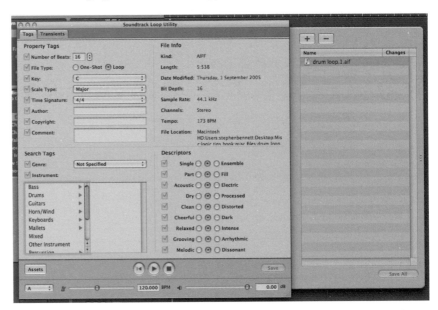

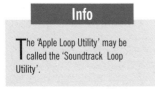

Here, as an example, we can create an Apple loop from a 4 bar recording of a drum kit. The original tempo is 130 bpm.

First load in the audio file. Click on the + in the file management (Assets) window. If it's not visible, click on the Assets button at the bottom left of the Apple Loops utility. Once the file is loaded, you can fill in the Tag fields. In this example we might set;

Number of beats =16
File type = loop
Key = none (as it's a percussion loop)
Scale= Neither (as it's a percussion loop)
Time signature =4/4
And so on.

Figure 8.5

The Transients pane

In a percussion-based audio file, you may not know the tempo of the file. The transients pane can be used to determine tempo from the 'beats' in the file.

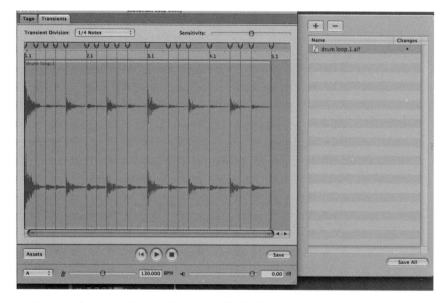

Figure 8.6

Tip

You can also use the BPM counter plug-in to determine an audio files tempo. Just insert it on the audio Track the Region you want to find the Tempo is on and press play.

Figure 8.7

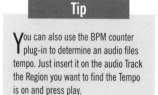

You can fine-tune the Apple loops utility's beat detection using the following parameters.

Transient division

A high beat value (1/8th notes or less) will mean fewer transients being detected. This is useful for slow tempo recordings.

A low beat value (1/6th notes or higher) will mean more transients being detected. This is useful for faster tempo recordings.

Sensitivity slider

This sets the amplitude or volume that the software will detect as being a transient. Low sensitivity means less transients being detected – i.e. only loud beats pass though.

Transients detected can be edited directly in the Transients pane. You can also add new transient information if the automatic system isn't suitable (for non- percussive audio files)

Adding a transient

Click in the area below the Transient division pull down menu.

Figure 8.8

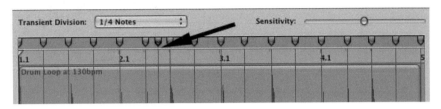

Moving a transient

Drag the marker in the below the Transient division pull down menu.

Deleting a transient

Drag the marker out of the area below the Transient division pull down menu, or select it and press Delete.

You can play back, and check out the effects of tempo changes of a created Apple loop.

Saving an Apple loop

Once you have created your loop, save it using the program's 'Save' button. Remember to save in the /library/Application Support/GarageBand directory if you want to audition the loop in the Apple loop browser.

Mixing

Mixing is a very important part of Logic these days. Many users mix entirely within Logic. This chapter aims to provide tips and methodology that will help in the mixing process.

Track mixer

This is the heart of the Logic mixer. It's a visible representation of all the Tracks that are on the Arrange page.

Figure 9.1

Figure 9.2

You can see down the left hand side of the Track mixer you can show and hide various Objects from the Track mixer.

Normally, you would only have MIDI, Virtual Instrument and Audio Tracks in the Arrange page when working on a Song – but you'll want Auxes, Busses and the Master output channel in the Track mixer. You may expect these to appear in the

Figure 9.3

Track mixer when you use the Track mixer buttons. But this will only happen if these objects are in the Arrange page too.

To make Auxes and Busses (and other Objects, such as Arpeggiators) appear in the Arrange page (and thus the Track mixer, you need to make sure the box next to the Icon in the Object Parameter box on the Environment page is ticked.

Then you can insert the required Auxes and Busses in the Arrange Page. These will then appear in the Track mixer too.

The master output channel can be added to the Arrange page in the same way. This controls the overall output level in Logic, so it's an essential addition!

Figure 9.4

Creating Track Mixer Groups

The Track mixer shows all the Tracks on the Arrange page and it can get very big in horizontal direction in a large Song. You can create Track mixer 'groups' by using Folders in the Arrange page.

Figure 9.5

Choose the Arrange page menu item, Region>Folder>Pack Folder to create a folder in the Arrange page.

Double click on the Folder to open it.

Create the Tracks you want to have in a group in the Folder. In this example, it's all the audio Tracks used to play back a Drum kit recording.

Close the Folder using the box at the top left of the Arrange page.

Create another folder. This time it's for backing vocals.

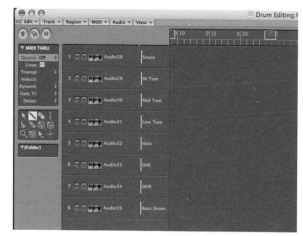

Figure 9.6

Figure 9.7

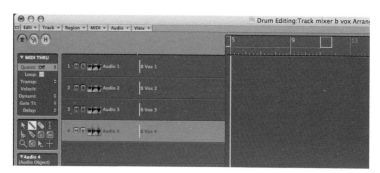

Figure 9.8

Arrange as Screenset with the following layout. Hold the Option key when you open the Track mixer from the Windows menu to keep the Track mixer on top.

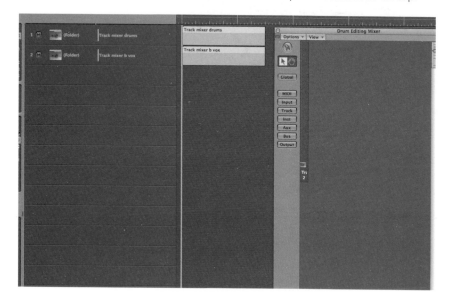

Figure 9.9

Figure 9.10

Check the Catch icon in the Track mixer.

Now, when you double click on the Folder in the Arrange page, the Track mixer will change to reflect the Tracks in the Folder. Here's the result of clicking on the Drums Folder.

Figure 9.11

And the backing vocals Folder.

Figure 9.12

Repeat for any other Track mixer configurations you require.

Grouping Track Mixer channels together

You may want to adjust the levels of some tracks together. You can group several objects together so that moving one of their faders will move all those in the same group and the same relative levels will be kept

To assign a group to a Track, use the Group pull down menu.

Figure 9.13

Figure 9.14

You can see what group is selected on the Group display.

Figure 9.15

If you open the Group settings window

Figure 9.16

You can name the group (i.e. Drum 'Subgroup', 'Guitars' etc.).

Choose what is to be grouped. For example, you could group sends to a bus (for reverb) or Arrange page automatic zooming as well as faders and pans.

Now we can insert EQ and plug-ins. Note in Figure 9.15 that the tracks 5 and 6 send their outputs to buss 2, which has a compressor and Emagic's PlatinumVerb Reverb as plug-ins. The volume slider of buss 2 will then control the outputs of all these tracks. Note also that tracks 7 and 8 have sends to buss 1. Buss 1 also has

Tip

Groups can be temporarily enabled and disabled by using a Key command. Disabling a group allows you to change the relative values of faders and so on in the group. Re-enabling the group re-instates the group movements. This is called the Group 'clutch'.

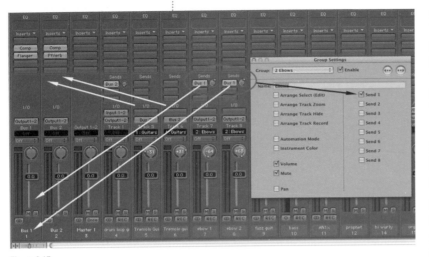

Figure 9.17

compression alongside a flanger. The level slider on buss 1 now acts as a return level for these effects to be blended in with Tracks 7 and 8. You can see that these sends are linked in the 'Ebows' group.

Displaying a lot of channels in the Track mixer on a small screen

If you have a lot of Tracks in your Song it can become tedious to scroll along a long list of Track mixer faders. To get around this, open two Track mixers, use the Windows>Tile Windows horizontally menu item to place them on the screen as in the next figure. Now you can show the first group of Tracks in the top window, the rest in the bottom window.

Figure 9.18

Resetting parameters to default values and resetting faders to 0

You can reset any fader or pan pot (and most values in some plug-ins) to their default values by holding down the Option key and clicking on the control.

Dragging plug-ins

You can drag plug-ins around in the Track Mixer by selecting the hand tool and dragging them to a new Track or another slot on the same Track. If you hold down the Option key you can copy the Plug-in along with all its settings. This is an easy way to set up similar plug-ins on several similar tracks.

Figure 9.19

You can also drag and copy plug-ins on the Arrange page Channel Strip. Of course, here you can only copy to another plug-in slot.

If you have a two-button mouse, you can use the right mouse key to select the hand tool.

Sends and Busses

If you have multiple Tracks, for example 7 drum Tracks, you may want to add a reverb to all of them to get a specific ambience, or put a compressor across the whole drum kit. Adding the same reverb and compressor to all the Tracks is possible but inefficient – it uses up a lot of CPU power. It's often better to use a single plug-in to process many Tracks rather than use an individual one on each Track. We can do this using a Bus. First create a Bus in the Environment then choose it in the Arrange page.

> **Tip**
>
> To gain even more screen space, hide the Track mixer parameters box from the View menu.

> **Tip**
>
> If you want values on your Track mixer faders to be in dB rather than displayed numerically you can from the Track Parameter box.

Figure 9.20

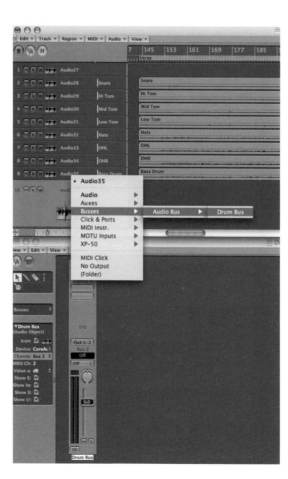

Figure 9.21

Figure 9.22

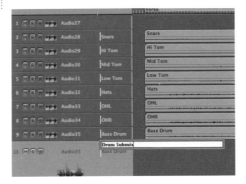

Position the Bus under the Drum Tracks. Give it a name – it's called Drum Submix' here. In this example we are using Bus 2.

Open the Track mixer. You'll see the 7 drum Tracks and the Bus here.

Figure 9.23

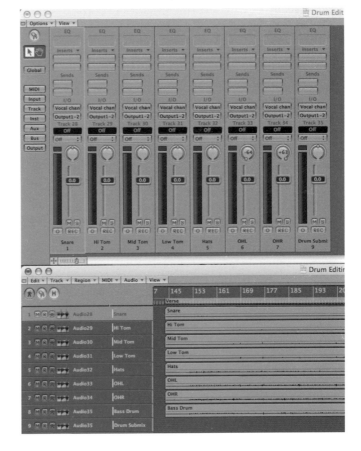

Figure 9.24

Insert your reverb and compressor on the Bus.

Now, send the output of each drum Track to the Bus.

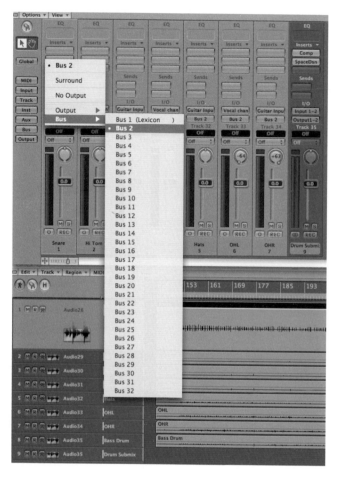

Figure 9.25

Now the Audio from each Track is being routed to the Bus and thus through the reverb and compressor.

Bringing external hardware into Logic

Although it's possible to record and mix entirely in Logic using it's own and third party plug-ins, many people want to use their old synthesisers and effects units too.

Live Inputs and External instruments

If you have a soundcard or interface with multiple inputs, you can route the outputs from an external synthesiser or mixing desk back into Logic Pro. These inputs can then be incorporated with audio tracks and virtual instruments when bouncing down, eliminating the use of an external mastering machine, such as DAT or Tape.

Live inputs are just another Audio object. Here's how you use them in Logic.

Create an Audio object from the Environment page New>Audio object menu item or from the Arrange page Track>Create multiple..... .Menu item.

Now choose a mono or stereo input via the channel Parameter. These inputs

Tip

Busses can be sent to Busses for further routing combinations.

Info

Using Busses and Auxes have latency implications. See the section on Plug-in Delay Compensation (PDC) below.

represent the physical inputs on your interface. The examples here are inputs 5 and 6. You could rename this object to 'FX return' or 'Roland Jupiter 8 input' for example.

If you are returning the sound from an effects unit, such as a reverb, you'll obviously need to send the audio to the unit from somewhere within Logic. The best way to do this is to use a Bus Audio object.

First create an Audio object from the New>Audio object Environment menu item. Now select a Bus object from the Channel parameter list. Make sure it's a stereo bus if you have a stereo FX unit. Rename the object 'Bus FX send'.

Figure 9.26

Figure 9.27

Select the outputs you have the external FX unit connected to. Say outputs 5 and 6 as previously. Now, if you send to this bus from an audio track, the Bus acts as a send to the external FX, while the live inputs are a return.

Figure 9.28 (left)

Figure 9.29

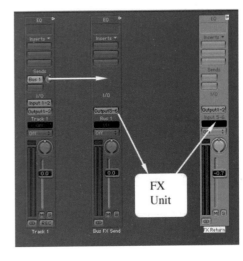

If you open the Audio>Audio configuration window, you can name the inputs, outputs and sends. Select the View menu item>I/O labels.

You can now rename the various sends, inputs and outputs.

Figure 9.30

You can also name any input, outputs or busses on your system.

Figure 9.31

You can also send directly to outputs and return to inputs on a channel using the I/O plug-in

Setup a MIDI Multi Instrument object from the Environment New>Multi

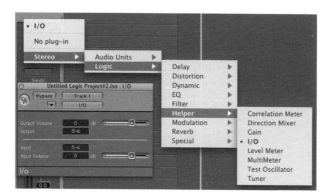

Figure 9.32

Instrument menu item. Connect it to the MIDI port the effects unit connected to. You can then name and change patches on the external effects unit.

You can add Virtual effect plug-ins to Live inputs. However, there are latency issues here. See the section on Plug-in Delay Compensation (PDC) later in this chapter.

External instruments

These are specialized versions of Live inputs. You can route the outputs from your external hardware (Synthesisers etc) to the inputs of your Audio interface and then onto the Arrange page in Logic. The advantage of the External Instrument is that the sound from the hardware device can be easily bounced down during a real-time mix along with Virtual instruments and Audio tracks. You could also return hardware effects units through an External instruments track.

Here's how you set them up.

Select or create an Audio Instrument object.

Instance the External plug-in from the pull down menu.

Figure 9.33

Select a MIDI instrument from the pull down menu.

Figure 9.34

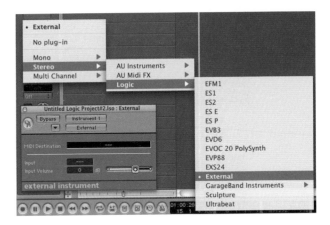

You can see that the External Instrument looks exactly like a Virtual instrument track.

Figure 9.35

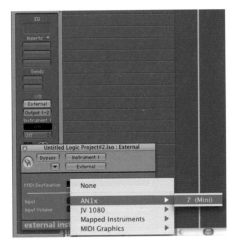

Tip

You can also add effects plug-ins to the External Instrument.

Figure 9.36

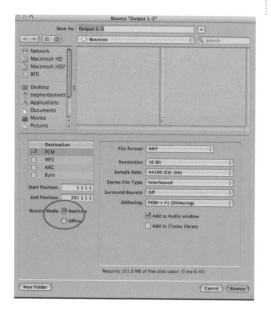

Figure 9.37

Tip

If you return any external Effects or Synthesiers through Logic's External Instrument or Live inputs, any Latency will be compensated for by PDC. See the section on Plug-in Delay Compensation.

Tip

When bouncing down a Song with External Instruments or other audio coming in through Input objects or the I/O plug-in, you must use Real Time bouncing.

Hide tracks

If you have a complex Arrange page with many Tracks, you may find yourself running out of screen 'real estate'. You can Hide tracks by making sure the 'H' button is ON and using the Arrange page>View>Hide Current Track and Select next Track menu item. Toggling the 'H' button on and off hides and shows the Tracks.

Figure 9.38

Side chains

Some plug-ins can be affected or controlled from another channel via their plug-in side chains. A side-chain input allows a plug-in to be controlled by another audio source. You could, for example, use a voice track to adjust a compressor on a music track causing the music to drop as the person speaks. Or you can use a complex rhythmic part to control a gate for 'chopping effects. Here, we're attempting to tighten up a bass synthesiser part by inserting a gate on the bass track and sending a bass drum signal through a side-chain to the gate.

Figure 3.39

The drum loop is on Audio Track 1, the bass on Audio Track 2. Insert a gate on the bass track.

Figure 9.40

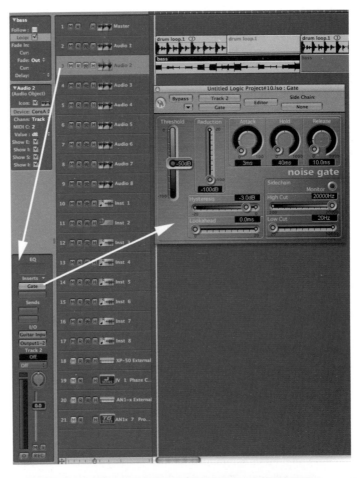

Figure 9.41

Select the side chain input from Track 1 (Audio 1).

Now on playback, the drum loop will control the gate.

> **Tip**
>
> Logic's Compressor, Expander, Noise Gate, Silver Compressor, and Silver Gate all have side chain inputs.

Other uses of side chains in Logic

- Autofilter. You can use a signal on the side chain of the autofilter to adjust the modulation of the filter. If you use a percussive input, the filter cutoff frequency will be modulated in time with the song.

Figure 9.42

- Fuzz-wah. The side chain input is used to control the motion of the wah-wah filter. If you set side chain input to the same Track on which the Fuzz-Wah is instanced will produce a true auto-wah effect.

Figure 9.43

• Ringshifter. When using this plug-in in Ring Modulator mode, you can use the side chain as the modulating signal, rather than it's internal LFO. This produces a more complex output.

Figure 9.44

Info

The EVOC PS Vocoder also has a side chain input. This is covered in Chapter 5.

• Match EQ. This EQ uses a recording you wish to copy the EQ from and imposes the copied EQ onto a destination file. You can send the template spectrum though the side chain to Match EQ.

Figure 9.45

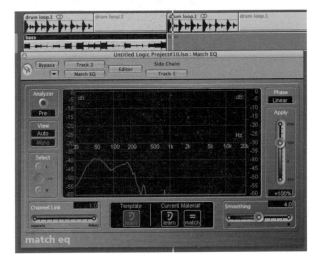

Plug-in Delay Compensation (PDC)

Latency, and its effect on Logic was discussed in Chapter 4. Logic has PDC to compensate for the latencies that occur when audio passes through various parts of Logic. The figure below shows how audio may pass through Logic.

Each different path will impart different amounts of delay. One plug-in or Virtual instrument will have a different latency than another. There will also be delays when audio passes through multiple Busses and Auxes. Logic uses PDC to overcome this problem.

Correctly written plug-ins will pass their latency value through to Logic and Logic will delay various parts of the recording so everything lines up.

Logic has three PDC settings. These are selected in the general section of the Audio Preferences.

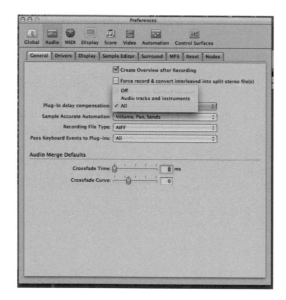

Figure 9.46

• Off. No latency compensation occurs. Use this setting if you are using Logic in the same way you would an old-style analog Tape Recorder and taking the tracks into a mixing desk. In this case, you won't be using plug-ins. Logic will not be delayed on playback.
• Audio tracks and instruments. Use this setting if you are not using Busses or Auxes.
• Full. Use this if you are using Busses and Auxes and mixing totally within Logic.

Using hardware controllers in Logic

If you have a hardware controller that can send out MIDI controller data from the controls, you can use these to control various parameters in Logic. These could be anything from the Modulation, Pitch bend wheels and Expression pedals on your synthesizer to a dedicated hardware box with lots of knobs, faders and switches. Some hardware controllers have 'pre-set' assignments within Logic.

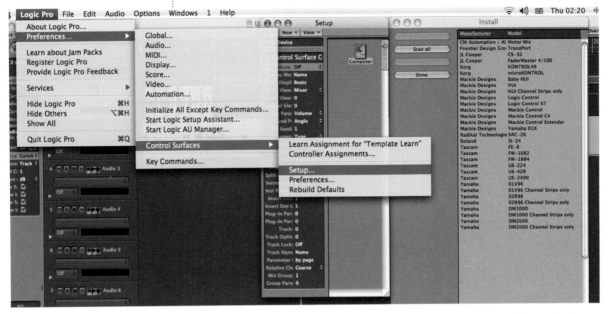

Figure 9.47

However, you can easily allow your hardware controller control of any Logic on-screen parameter manually. You could, for example, use knobs on a synthesizer that send MIDI controllers to adjust parameters on the ES-1 Virtual instrument.

- Choose menu item Logic Pro > Preferences > Control Surfaces > Controller Assignments
- Click Learn Mode
- Move the on-screen knob you want to control – Pan knob on a Channel strip, for example
- Move the physical knob or slider you want to use on your hardware controller
- Repeat steps 3 and 4 as necessary

Automation quick access

You can quickly assign a control on a keyboard or MIDI mixer, as long as it puts out MIDI controller data when moved, to an Automation parameter. First you need to make sure that the Arrange page view>Track automation is turned ON and that the Parameter you wish to learn is chosen from the Track automation list.

Figure 9.48

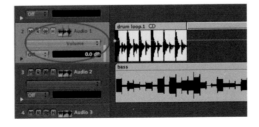

To use automation Quick Access, open it from the Main page Options>Track Automation Settings. Click on 'Assign' when asked.

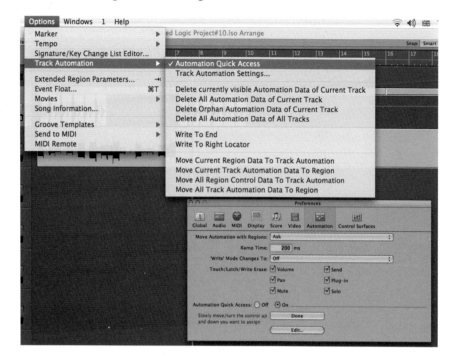

Figure 9.49

Click on 'Learn Message' and slowly move your hardware control. This could be a modulation wheel, a pedal knob or a slider. In this example, it's the Modulation wheel (which puts out controller number 2).

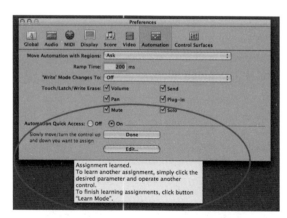

Figure 9.50

Logic will tell you the Assignment has been learned. Click on 'Done'. If you click on 'Edit....' A window opens (Figure 9.51). Deselect the Learn Mode button. You can see that Controller 2 is set to Volume automation.

Figure 9.51

Panning

Each Audio, MIDI and Virtual instrument has a Pan control. You can determine the mode in which the Panning will operate from the File>Song Settings>Audio preferences window.

Figure 9.52

There are three options:

- 0dB – mono signals seem louder when set to the centre position and quieter at the extreme left and right pans.
- -3dB – the level of the signal at the centre position is 3dB less than when the Pan Law is set to 0dB.
- -3dB compensated – the level of the signal at the centre position is the same as the 0dB setting. However when the pan control is set to full left or right pan positions they will be 3dB louder than the 0dB setting.

Creating 'Doubled' parts

It's often useful to record a part twice and then hard pan the first recording to the left and the second to the right. This gives the recording a fuller and wider image. This is especially useful on guitar recordings.

You can simulate this effect with one recording in the following way. Record the part.

Figure 9.53

Copy it to another Track (hold down the Option key while dragging.)

Figure 9.54

Figure 9.55

Pan the two Regions to the left and right.
Select the first copy and set a delay time of +25 in the Region parameter box.

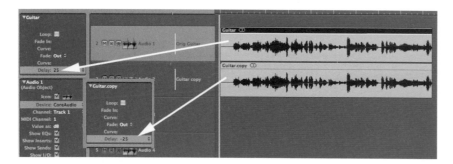

Figure 9.56

Repeat with the second Region but set the delay to −25 on this one.

Figure 9.57

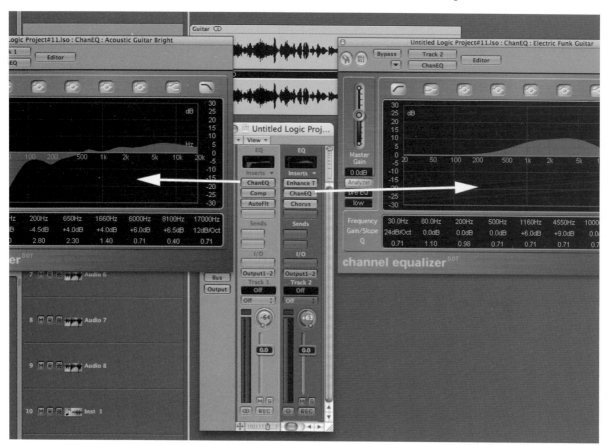

Creating harmonies from a single recording.

You can use a similar technique to create harmonies. Record a vocal part. Copy it to another Track. Instance the AUPitch plug-in on the second Track. Change the pitch of the second Track to get the harmony you desire.

Figure 9.58

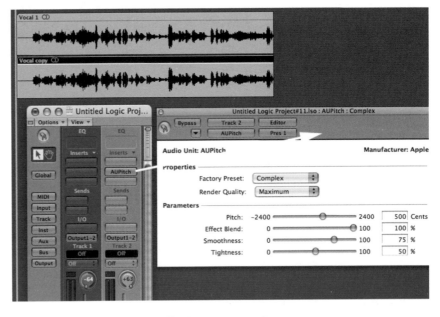

Tip

Improve the harmonies by using the Region parameter delay function, EQ, Compression and Chorus plug-ins.

Repeat with as many other Tracks as you require.

Where are my Plug-in slots, Sends and Auxes?

Figure 9.59

You'll notice that Logic's Channel Strip only has two Insert slots and two sends by default. As you use up these slots, a new one will be created.

In a similar fashion, if you are creating Auxes in the Environment, there only appears to be 3 available. Again, as you use these Auxes, more will become available.

Automation

Logic has an extensive and fully featured automation system. Everything can be automated; levels, pans, sends, plug-in parameters, Solo and Muting. This makes it ripe for a section of automation tips and tricks.

Figure 9.60

Automation preferences

The automation preferences window can be accessed from the main Logic Preferences menu or the Options>Track Automation Settings menu.

There are several preferences available.

Figure 9.61

Move automation with Regions

This has three settings, Never, Always and Ask. Ask is probably the most useful setting as you'll almost always want to choose whether you want to move the automation data or not.

Ramp time

When you are using automation in Touch mode, this parameter defines how long it takes for an automation curve to return to the previously recorded values after you stop moving a control.

Figure 9.62

- Write mode changes to: This is the mode the Track will change to after you have finished recording automation onto a Track. If you set this to Read, it will stop you accidentally overwriting any previous data.
- Touch/latch/Write Erase: Here you can define which parameters can be changed when you use these automation modes. You'd normally leave all these boxes ticked.
- Automation quick access: This is discussed earlier in this Chapter.

Automation Display preferences

There are a couple of display-based preferences that relate to automation. They are in the Display preference's Arrange section.

You can define the transparency of the Regions (objects) and the associated automation data (other). This can make it easier to see the automation on a Track. To see this effect, you need to have a high zoom setting.

Figure 9.63

Figure 9.64

Tip

You can edit any automation data on a Track in the Event List editor by using the Automation Event Edit Key Command.

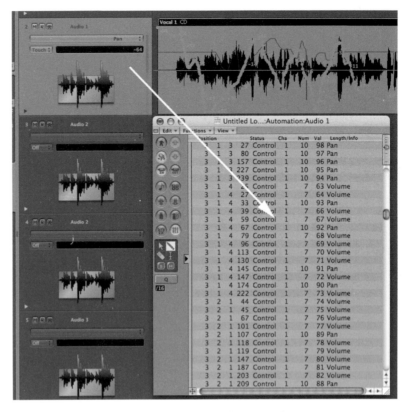

Figure 9.65

Automation and the vocal track – Using the mouse for automation.

Automation has revolutionised the mixing process. You can fine-tune volume and other parameters to such an extent that you can easily eliminate or suppress faults in the recording process – or with the person being recorded. Vocals are usually the most prominent feature in a song so it's vitally important that they sound right. We all know what a voice should sound like – we all have one! The following tips are all about creating the 'perfect' vocal track.

The first place to start is by removing any excessive breaths and other extraneous noises in between the actual singing lines using the mouse. The following figure is a typical vocal recording split it into individual phrases and compiled of various takes.

Figure 9.66

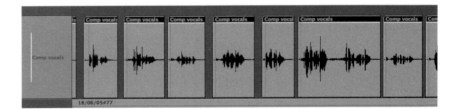

Figure 9.67

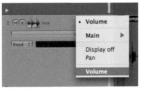

First, you need to make sure track automation is visible by using the Arrange page View, Track automation menu item. Now, select 'Volume' from the Automation data pull down menu. Also make sure the Automation mode is set to 'Read'.

You'll see the volume automation line appear. The easiest way to draw automation curves around these vocal phrases is to drag a box around them while holding down the Shift, Ctrl and Option keys simultaneously. On releasing the mouse, four automation nodes will be created. Repeat this for all the vocal phrases.

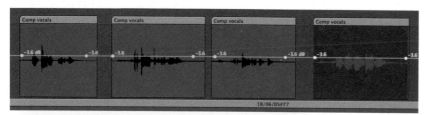

Figure 9.68

Figure 9.69

If you drag the line in between phrases down, you'll see volume curves created around each phrase.

Now you can use the mouse to edit this data. If you zoom the track or the window you can see the curves in more detail. Nodes can be dragged around using the mouse. You can also use 'S' shaped curves (chosen from the drop down menu under the Toolbox. Once you have volume automation curves around each phrase you can do some finer editing.

Removing or lowering breath noises

You can change the feel of a vocal recording by lowering or completely removing the vocalists breathing – especially noticeable if you're using a compressor plug-in on the voice. Breaths at the start of phrases are dealt with by the method described above – just move the start curve of the automation 'islands' until the breath is cut out. If you have a breath within a phrase, you'll probably want to work in a slightly different way.

Drag a box around the breath noise while holding down the Shift, Ctrl and Option keys simultaneously to create four nodes.

Now drag down the line between the nodes. You'll probably find that removing the breath within a phrase completely will sound unnatural, so you may just want to reduce the level a little.

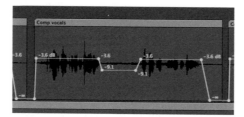

Figure 9.70

You can now drag nodes around to fine-tune where the volume drop goes.

Reducing the effects of plosives and sibilance

These are the bane of vocal recordings. You can always use a hardware or software de-esser to try and remove sibilance, but these can often sound unnatural. With total automation available, you can deal with each case by reducing the volume for a small

Figure 9.71

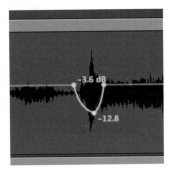

period of time at the point of the offending sibilance or plosive. Listen through to the vocal track in solo mode and at a high on-screen zoom magnification. When you reach a sibilant 'S' or a popping 'P', stop the sequencer. Create three nodes by clicking just before and after the area and one inside these two nodes. Drag down the middle node.

You need to listen to the automation to make sure you haven't gone too far. You'll probably need to finely edit the start end and drop of the automation too. S-shaped curves are also useful in this situation, as they seem to help in getting a more naturalistic effect.

The drop in volume only needs to be of the order of milliseconds to reduce the effect of sibilance or pops – any more and you'll hear definite volume drops. Using this method on sibilance keeps the track sounding bright and doesn't produce that 'toothless' effect that de-essers can sometimes cause. It's hard work but rewarding. Of course, you may have to modify this automation further later in the mix process – automation can rarely be done in isolation.

You can use this technique for any track that needs fine volume editing - and not just volume. If you look at the Track automation list automation pull-down menu you'll see the automatable

Figure 9.72

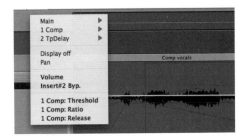

parameters of all the plug-ins on a track along with volume, pan, solo, mute, any sends and effects bypass. This latter one is particularly useful if you want a plug-in to only affect part of a track. You can add echo just to the end of vocal phrases by un-bypassing an effect at a particular point in the track. Some plug-ins can cause pops when you do this. If this is the case, insert the plug-in on a bus and automate the send to that bus instead.

Figure 9.73

It's easy to see how powerful this technique is. Another thing to try are to adjust the output, ratio and threshold of a compressor during a song to help the vocal sit in the mix. It's also easy to increase sends to delays or reverbs when a mix gets busy and reduce the levels for a drier sound during sparser sections.

While it may seem more natural to use Logic's automation system with a hardware controller or on-screen knobs, the mouse-based editing features are essential for fine-tuning and so shouldn't be overlooked.

Stem mixing

One of the annoying limitations of Logic's automation system is that there is no way to increase or reduce all automation data in one go. Consider a typical mixing scenario you've adjusted all your backing tracks until you're happy with the mix, but you need a few extra dB on vocals and bass drum. However, just raising the levels of these tracks takes the master over 0dB. What you really want to do is lower all the other tracks proportionally instead. To do this, you'll have to lower the volume *and, perhaps, other automation data* on each track! Imagine how long this would take if you have 48 tracks with complex and multiple automation data! The section 'Editing automation data with the mouse', below, lists various mouse-based commands that can help to make this easier, but you may also want to think of mixing using the 'stem' technique.   What this means in practice is sending several similar tracks to busses. You could, for example, send all the drums to one bus, backing vocals to another, guitars to another and so on. Balancing would then be just a matter of adjusting the level of these busses rather than overall tracks –and you can automate these busses too. Individual 'stems' can be compressed individually – which also helps in getting things to 'sit in the mix'. Of course, you will still have to edit other automation data, such as a synthesisers' filter cut-off individually for each track – but you're unlikely to want to do this simultaneously on many instruments.

Editing automation data with the mouse

The way nodes and lines are created and edited in Logic are affected with modifier keys. Here's a handy list of these.

Tip

You need to use the Arrow tool unless stated otherwise to perform these operations.

Creating automation nodes with the Arrow Tool

Add a new node by a short click anywhere on the Track.

Add a new node on an existing line with a short click on the automation line.

To create 4 nodes around a part of a region hold down the Shift, Ctrl and Alt keys and rubberband the area you wish to create nodes over. See the main body for information about a bug with this under Logic 7.1.

To create 2 nodes around a part of a region hold down the Shift and Alt keys and rubberband the area you wish to create nodes over.

Selecting Automation data with the Arrow tool

Select a node by clicking and holding on node. A little info window will appear giving you details about the node.

Select a line by clicking and holding on the line.

Selecting a group of nodes

Hold down the Shift key and rubberband around the nodes. You must do this within the boundary of a region; otherwise you'll select the region itself. You can then move the whole selection by dragging the lines or the nodes within the selection.

To select all Automation from nearest node to the song's end, Hold down the Alt key and click on the node.

To select all Automation on a track, hold down the Alt key and DOUBLE click on a node.

Selecting automation nodes with the Automation Tool set to 'Select'.

To select ALL the automation on a region just click on the region.

To select non-continuous areas & extend areas, hold down the Shift key and rubberband each area.

De-selecting automation nodes

To de-select ALL automation, click outside the track.

Moving automation

To move single nodes just click and drag a node.

To move single automation lines, just click and drag the line.

To move a selection of nodes horizontally (forwards/backwards in time), click-hold and drag a line or node.

To move a selection of nodes vertically (increment or decrement), click-hold and drag a line or node.

Moving automation with the Automation tool set to 'curve'.

In this mode, dragging a line will result in a curve. Depending on where you drag the line, the curve will be either a 'smile' shape or 'S' shaped. You can do this with the Arrow tool while holding down the Alt and Control keys and a long click on the line.

Scaling automation data

To scale selected automation data up and down (increment or decrement) proportionally, click-hold and drag NOT on a Line or Node. To do this to a whole tracks' visible data, hold down the Command key and drag the level slider to the right of the Instrument column up or down.

Copying automation data

To copy a selection of automation data with the Arrow Tool, hold down the Alt key, and click-hold and drag the selection.

Deleting automation data

Delete a node with a short click on the node.

To delete selected Automation data use the backspace key (but check no objects are selected as well!)

To delete all Automation data of track hold down the Shift and Alt keys and Double click on the track.

Tip

If you hold down the Command key and drag the meter on the Track up and down, this moves all the visible automation data up or down.

Figure 9.74

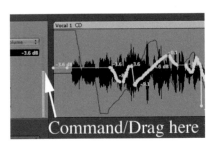

Inserting a reverb or delay plug-in on a bus – the wet/dry setting

When you use a Tracks Send control to route audio to a Bus with a reverb or delay plug-in inserted, you are effectively bleeding off a little of the Audio passing through that Track and mixing the effected signal in with the dry signal passing through the Track.

In these cases you should set the 'Dry' or 'Direct' signal to zero and the 'Reverb' or 'Wet' or Mix control to its fullest extent.

Figure 9.75

Figure 9.76

Pre and Post Sends

You can choose between these modes on a Track objects' Send controls.

- Post. The Send knob is connected to the Channel strip's volume control. This means that when you reduce the level on the Track, the send level reduces at the same level thus maintaining the relative level of the effect.
- Pre. In this case, when you reduce the volume fader the effect on the Bus remains the same. It's really useful as an effect or for setting up monitor mixes where you can send signals to monitors without the main volumes being up.

Pre Fader metering

When this is ON, the level of the Track is still displayed even if the volume slider is on zero.

MIDI Mixing tips

External MIDI equipment

TYou may want to record external synthesizer sounds that are being played back by MIDI by Logic's sequencer as Audio Tracks. You can do this in two ways:

Route the synthesizer out into Logic via a recording Track and record as normal.

Route the synthesizer into Logic using an External Instrument, solo the track and bounce it down in Realtime.

Figure 9.77

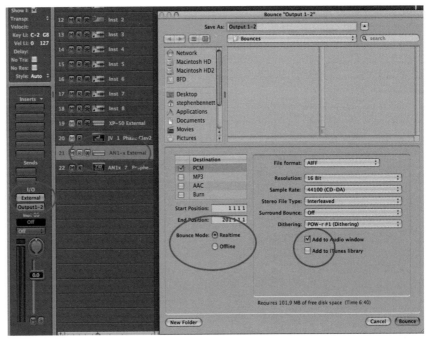

Figure 9.78

Re-import the bounced file and drag it from the Audio window to line up with the original MIDI data.

MIDI Compression

Figure 9.79

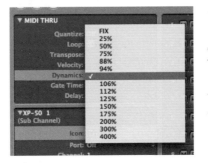

The dynamics parameter in the Region Parameter box is a sort of 'compressor' for MIDI data. Hold the mouse key down to change the values from a pop up menu. This parameter changes the differences between the softest and loudest velocity values in a Region. Values over 100% expand the dynamic range of the values, increasing the difference between the softest and loudest velocity values, while those less than 100% decrease the difference, or compress, the values.

Some mixing tips using Logic's plug-ins

Processing drums

Individual drums may require different effects. In addition the whole kit, or sections of the kit can also be processed with the same effects.

Tip

These tips can also be used on sampled or synthesised drums.

Processing the bass drum

- EQ. Try cutting or boosting the frequency at about 300Hz by about 10dB. This should clear up any muddiness in the sound. You may also want to boost the high frequencies at around 5000 to 6000Hz if the drum sounds really dull. Boosting the frequency at around 40 to 100Hz, perhaps as a shelf EQ, will add weight to the sound.

Tip

Adjusting the Q control changes the range of frequencies the EQ affects. You'll need to adjust these parameters by ear.

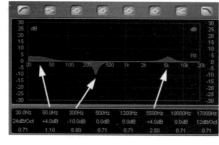

Figure 9.80

Compression

The bass drum is often the main pulse of a song, so it's important that its level is even. If you are finding that the level varies a lot, try the following settings on a compressor.

- Ratio. For a mild compression effect set the ratio at 4:1. For a more aggressive effect set it to 10:1
- Attack. Set this to 1 to 5 ms or fast. This means the signal is affected quickly – i.e. the compressor works right away to keep sound level in volume. This is particularly important with percussive sounds.
- Release. Set this to around 0.2s. You'll need to experiment with this value. If the sound starts to 'pump', or jump rapidly up and down in level, reduce the value.
- Threshold. Turn down the threshold control until the compressor starts to work (you'll see the gain reduction in the meter on the compressor). Further reduce the control until you get a nice level sound.
- Gain make up. Increase the value of the gain make up control until the bass drum is at the same level as the non-compressed sound.

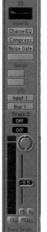

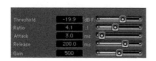

Figure 9.81

- Gate. You can isolate each bass drum hit by gating the individual hits. You'll have to do this by ear. Solo the bass drum and adjust the threshold and attack and release controls of the gate until you only hear the bass drum.
- Pan. Pan the bass drum to the centre.

Figure 9.82

Tip

Keep bypassing the EQ and compressor to see what effect they are having on the sound and to set the processed level to the same as the unprocessed one.

Tip

You may want to keep de-soloing the individual drums so you can hear them in context as you process.

Figure 9.83

Processing the snare drum

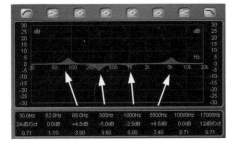

- EQ. Try boosting the frequency at
  about 5000Hz to 6000Hz to add
  a bit of brightness to the sound.
  You can 'thicken' up the snare by
  boosting a few dB at around
  60Hz to 100Hz. If the snare
  sounds muddy try a cut at around
  300Hz. If the snare sounds too
  harsh, try cutting a few dB at 1000Hz.

Compression

Try these settings as a starting point.

- Ratio. For a mild compression effect set the ratio at 4:1. For a more aggressive
  effect set it to 10:1
- Attack. Set this to 1 to 5 ms or fast. This means the signal is affected quickly –
  i.e. the compressor works right away to keep sound level in volume.
- Release .Set this to around 0.2s. You'll need to experiment with this value. If
  the sound starts to 'pump' reduce the value.
- Threshold. Turn down the threshold control until the compressor starts to work
  (you'll see the gain reduction in the meter on the compressor). Further reduce
  the control until you get a nice level sound.
- Gain make up. Increase the value of the gain make up control until the snare
  drum is at the same level as the non-compressed sound.
- Gate. You can isolate each snare drum hit by gating the individual hits in the
  same ways as the bass drum.
- Pan. Pan the snare to the same position it was when recording. Usually the
  snare sits slightly to the left of the drummer from their perspective. So to hear
  it from a listener's point of view, pan it slightly to the right.

Overhead microphones

You'll treat the two overhead tracks in exactly the same way – as a stereo recording.

Figure 9.84

- EQ. Try boosting the overheads
  at around 10000Hz to add
  brightness – try using a slope
  filter. You may also want to roll
  off the low end to reduce the
  effect of the bass and/or snare
  drums in the overheads.

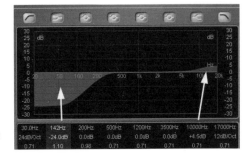

Compression

At this stage, just add a gentle
compression to the overheads.

- Ratio. For a mild compression effect set the ratio at 2:1 or 4:1
- Attack. Set this to 1 to 5 ms or fast. This means the signal is affected quickly –
  i.e. the compressor works right away to keep sound level in volume.

- Release. Set this to around 0.2s. You'll need to experiment with this value. If the sound starts to 'pump' reduce the value.
- Threshold. Turn down the threshold control until the compressor starts to work (you'll see the gain reduction in the meter on the compressor). Further reduce the control until you get a nice level sound.
- Gain make up. Increase the value of the gain make up control until the overheads are at the same level as the non-compressed sound.
- Pan. Pan the overhead tracks hard left and right. Remember; the listener will hear the opposite panning that the drummer hears, so pan the left overhead hard right and vice-versa.

Processing the whole drum mix

We'll use a Bus to process the whole drum mix. This Bus will allow us to adjust the level of the whole kit using one fader.

- Create or select a Bus. Make sure it is a stereo Bus.
- Make sure the outputs of the individual drum tracks run through the Bus rather than going straight to the Master outputs.

Now the fader, solo and mute buttons on the Bus will affect the all 4 of the drum tracks at the same time.

Figure 9.85

Figure 9.86

Compressing the whole drum track

A lot of modern music uses heavily compressed drums. How much you use on a whole drum sub-mix depends on the type of track you are producing.

Insert a compressor on the Bus. Try these settings as a starting point.

- Ratio. For a mild compression effect set the ratio at 4:1. For a more aggressive effect set it to 10:1
- Attack. Set this to 1 to 5 ms or fast. This means the signal is affected quickly – i.e. the compressor works right away to keep sound level in volume.
- Release. Set this to around 0.2s. You'll need to experiment with this value. If the sound starts to 'pump' reduce the value – unless this is the effect you want!
- Threshold. Turn down the threshold control until the compressor starts to work (you'll see the gain reduction in the meter on the compressor). Further reduce the control until you get a nice level sound. If you want a heavily compressed sound, pull the fader down more.
- Gain make up. Increase the value of the gain make up control until the drum sub-mix is at the same level as the non-compressed sound.

Figure 9.87

Processing guitars

Electric guitars

Figure 9.88

- EQ. Try boosting the frequency around 3000Hz to 6000Hz to brighten up a dull sound. Try cutting the same frequencies if you have a harsh sound. If the guitar sounds indistinct, try cutting the frequencies at 300Hz.

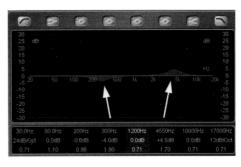

Compression

Electric guitars are often heavily compressed when recording. Depending on the type of music you are recording you may want to compress them some more. Try these settings as a starting point.

- Ratio. Try a compression ratio in the range 8:1 to 10:1
- Attack. Set this to 2 to 5 ms or fast. This means the signal is affected quickly – i.e. the compressor works right away to keep sound level in volume.
- Release. Set this to around 0.5s. You'll need to experiment with this value.
- Threshold. Turn down the threshold control until the compressor starts to work (you'll see the gain reduction in the meter on the compressor). Further reduce the control until you get a nice level sound.
- Gain make up. Increase the value of the gain make up control until the guitar is at the same level as the non-compressed sound.
- Pan. Panning guitars is an artistic decision. If you have two guitars or a guitar and a keyboard you may want to pan each slightly left and right.

Acoustic guitars

You can try the same EQ and compression settings on acoustic guitar as on the electric guitar. However, in general, you'll probably use less compression and a little frequency boost at around 2000Hz to 3000Hz to accentuate the plucked sound.

Processing bass

Figure 9.89

- EQ. For a deep, bassy sound try boosting a little around 40Hz. To reduce muddiness cut a little at 300Hz. You can even try adding boosting at 2000Hz to accentuate the 'twang'.

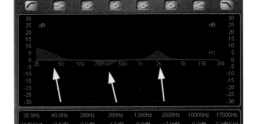

Compression

Try these settings as a starting point.

- Ratio. Try a compression ratio in the range 4:1 to 10:1
- Attack. Set this to 2 to 10 ms. A longer time produces a more 'compressed' sound. Very short attack can give the bass a distorted 'growl'.
- Release. Set this to around 0.5s. You'll need to experiment with this value. Often it's nice on bass to leave the compressor 'open', using a long release, to give the bass more sustain.
- Threshold. Turn down the threshold control until the compressor starts to work (you'll see the gain reduction in the meter on the compressor). Further reduce the control until you get a nice level sound.
- Gain make up. Increase the value of the gain make up control until the bass is at the same level as the non-compressed sound.
- Pan. Bass is usually panned in the centre along with the bass drum.

Keyboards

Keyboard instruments often have a wide frequency range that can interfere with other instruments and recordings. You may want to try cutting the low, mid and high frequencies, depending on the song. You can also boost the very highs for an 'airy' effect.

Keyboards are often in stereo so you can pan to any suitable point. See Panning tips below.

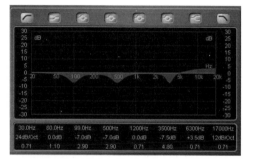

Figure 9.90

Panning tips

Panning places the sound in a position in the stereo field. You can use panning to position different elements of a mix in different position to increase clarity. In theory, you can pan any instrument anywhere. However, low frequency instruments such as bass drum or bass are usually panned to the centre, as are vocals. Judicious use of panning can help simulate the effect of a group of instruments spread out over the stereo field. You can also use panning as an effect – swinging the sound from one speaker to another.

Processing vocals

If your song has vocals, they will usually be the most important part of the arrangement. A poor vocal is the often main reason a recording can sound 'non professional'. Vocalists vary tremendously, as do the microphones used to record them. As vocals are the one instrument we all possess and can use to a greater or lesser extent, we are very sensitive to problems with recordings of the voice.

As well as the lead voice you may also have backing vocals, which are usually processed in a slightly different way to enhance their differences.

Processing backing vocals

Depending on what type of backing vocals you have, it may be a good idea to separate them in frequency from the lead vocal in the mix.

On each separate backing vocal track you can try:

Figure 9.91

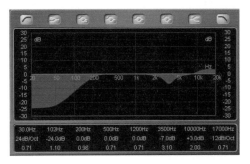

EQ Try boosting the upper frequencies, say at 10000Hz to make the vocal more airy. You may also want to reduce the low frequency content to accentuate this effect. If the vocals sound nasal, reduce the frequencies at 3000Hz to 4000Hz. Use a shelf filter to cut out low frequencies and traffic rumble noise.

Figure 9.92

Pan the backing vocals. Where you pan them depends on how many backing vocals you have recorded.

Send the backing vocals to a Bus in the same way as you did with the drum mix.

Now compress the backing vocal sub mix by inserting a compressor on the bus.

Try these settings as a starting point.

Figure 9.93

- Ratio. 4:1 to 10:1
- Attack. Set this to 2 to 5 ms or fast. This means the signal is affected quickly – i.e. the compressor works right away to keep sound level in volume.
- Release. Set this to around 0.3s. You'll need to experiment with this value.
- Threshold. Turn down the threshold control until the compressor starts to work (you'll see the gain reduction in the meter on the compressor). Further reduce the control until you get a nice level sound. If you want a heavily compressed sound, pull the fader down more.
- Gain make up. Increase the value of the gain make up control until the backing vocals are at the same level as the non-compressed sound.

Processing lead vocals

Try boosting a small amount at 5000Hz to 60000Hz. Be careful with increasing the high frequencies on vocals; this can lead to sibilance, especially on 's' words. Boosting the upper frequencies at about 10000Hz will make the vocal more airy. If the vocals sound nasal, reduce the frequencies at 3000Hz to 4000Hz. You may need to reduce the frequencies at around 300Hz to increase clarity. Use a shelf filter to cut out low frequency and rumble noise.

Figure 9.94

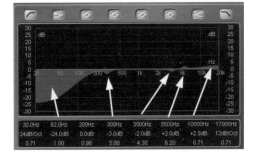

Compression

You can use a lot of different types of compression on vocals. If you have a vocalist with a wide dynamic range, you'll have to compress more to get the vocal to 'sit' in the mix. It's common to use a 'classic' compressor plug-in on vocals to enhance the sound further.

Try this range of settings as a starting point.

- Ratio. 2:1 to 10:1
- Attack. Set this to 2 to 5 ms or fast. This means the signal is affected quickly – i.e. the compressor works right away to keep sound level in volume.
- Release. Set this to around 0.3s to 0.5s. You'll need to experiment with this value.
- Threshold. Turn down the threshold control until the compressor starts to work (you'll see the gain reduction in the meter on the compressor). Further reduce the control until you get a nice level sound. If you want a heavily compressed sound, pull the fader down more.
- Gain make up. Increase the value of the gain make up control until the vocals are at the same level as the non-compressed sound.

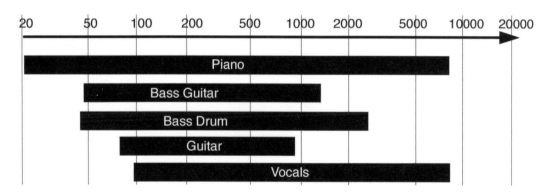

Frequency in Hz

Figure 9.95

Automation level adjustment versus compression

Using compression to maintain a constant level has a very specific effect that may or may not be suitable for a given occasion. Using automation produces a more 'natural' sound.

Making a vocal 'sit' in the mix

Vocal recordings that have no ambience can sound dull or dry. Many vocal recordings use reverb or delay to help make them sound more natural. If you use too long a reverb or delay time however, the vocal may sound drowned out and indistinct. As a rule of thumb, you can use a longer reverb or delay on slower tracks, with less on faster or more intimate ones. Long reverb or delay times will make the vocal sound distant, so it's logical that using short delays or reverbs will make them seem closer and more intimate.

To add reverb to a vocal track: Create a stereo Bus. Insert a reverb plug-in on the Bus. Select a suitable reverb.

Figure 9.96

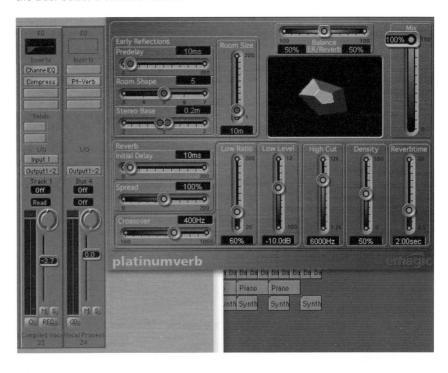

Set the wet/dry control to 100% wet (reverb). We want none of the 'dry' sound to pass through the bus. Leave the Bus level at 0 dB.

On the track mixer strip, use the send control to direct some of the signal to the Bus.

Adjust the level of the send so that it enhances the vocal sound. You may also want to try adjusting the pre-delay, the reverb time and high frequency filters to

make the reverb duller sounding compared to the unprocessed vocals. Too bright a reverb can cause excessive sibilance.

Now play back the track. Bring up send control to the Bus until you can just hear the reverb, then pull down the level of the send a little.

Figure 9.97

Figure 9.98

Mastering

Introduction

Mastering used to mean the process of preparing a tape recording for cutting onto vinyl. Mastering engineers with years of experience would prepare the tape with specialised EQ to fit the recording onto the disc. With the advent of CD and digital recording, Mastering has come to mean something quite different. Mastering may involve any or all of the following processes:

- Arranging each song in the correct order (Compiling).
- Level matching each song so that there are no jumps in volume between them.
- Fade in and fade out the songs, or use crossfades if you want the songs to blend into each other.
- Processing with broad range EQ, Compression and Limiting to add a professional 'sheen' to the recordings and to make them sound cohesive when listened to as a whole.
- Creating a Master CD-R from which you can produce normal audio CDs or further CD-Rs.

Mastering is often said to be the process whereby you can add the professional 'gloss' to a recording. It's usually seen as a kind of arcane art. However, Audio recording software offers us the tools to produce our own masters, using the same tools we used for recording and mixing. As with mixing, listening to your own CD collections is a good way to hear what a good mastered recording sounds like and to compare it with your own work.

You will often hear people say that you cannot do your own mastering – you really need to send your mixes to a specialist. While it is true that there are many talented people with esoteric equipment available at high cost, it is very possible for you to master your songs yourself. Mastering isn't magic; it's like any process of recording. You need to practice, experiment, listen and try and fail before you get a good 'ear'.

Tip

Leave your mixes for a while before you master them. It's always a good idea to lose some familiarity with the work – you need to try to look at it as if it was a new recording.

Info

Re-mastering is the process of taking old recordings and using digital technology and plug-ins to improve their sound for CD production.

Tip

You are unlikely to be able to have available a room for mastering your work that is acoustically perfect. So you'll need to become familiar with its quirks – in the same way as with mixing. Listen to lots of commercial CDs in the room you'll be mastering in and compare these to your mastering efforts. With care, you'll be able to adjust your mastering technique to produce similar high quality work.

Most of the tools you'll need are exactly the same as the ones you have used when recording and mixing. A large part of the mastering process will entail the use of these plug-ins. While you may want to use the plug-ins that came with your audio software, you may also be interested in purchasing third-party ones that are specifically designed for mastering.

Figure 10.1

Arranging the songs into the correct order

Let's say, for example, you have 10 songs to compile.

Create 10 audio tracks in your audio hardware. Make sure they are stereo tracks.

Load in each song file to each track. Drag them to the order you require.

The type of mastering processing required will depend on the songs themselves. Even if you have recorded and mixed all the songs in the same way you'll find that they vary quite a bit in volume and tone.

> ## Tip
> You may want to master each song separately and then arrange them into the correct order afterwards. This may also be a useful method if you are using plug-ins that require a lot of CPU power.

> ## Tip
> The order you put your songs onto a CD is an important part of creating a finished product. It's often a good idea to produce rough CDs of different running orders until you find an order you like.

Figure 10.2

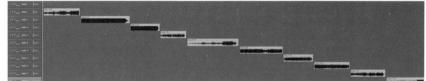

Adjusting the level

You can use Logic's automation to level match the tracks. If you listen to a few minutes of the end on one track through to the first few minutes of the next, you'll get an idea of the relative volume levels of the tracks.

You can then adjust the track levels using volume automation.

Figure 10.3

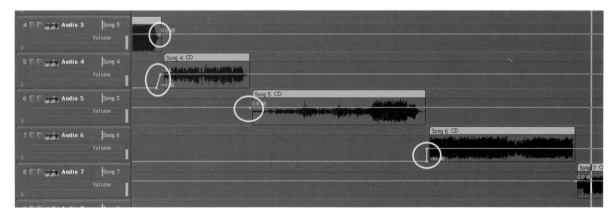

If you want track fade-ins and fade-outs you can use volume automation for this as well.

Figure 10.4

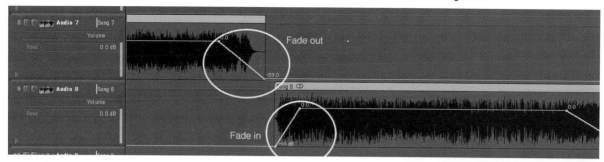

Crossfading from one track to another is also possible using volume automation.

Next, we'll want to process the songs with plug-ins. You don't always have to do this; processing isn't always needed. You may find that the mix sounds exactly the way you want it to as it is. In this case you can skip the processing section and jump right through to the 'Bouncing down the master' section.

However, most mixes will benefit from processing. You don't necessarily need to use all these plug-ins on every track. You'll need to make some creative decisions when listening to your songs.

There are two ways to master several songs for a complete CD.

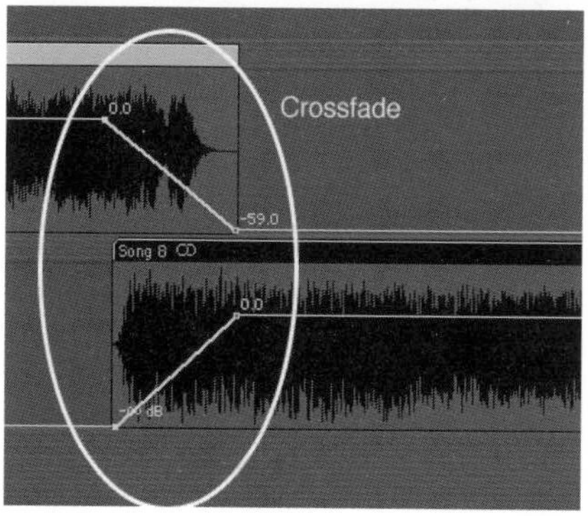

Figure 10.5

Processing each song individually

Each song will need to have the following processors inserted onto each individual track. Note that this method uses a lot of CPU power, as you will, in this example, need to have 10 of each of the plug-ins running at the same time.

> **Tip**
>
> Remember to keep bypassing the plug-in(s) to hear the effect they are having on the songs. Processing, especially boosting frequencies using EQ, will often increase the overall volume. This increase in volume can easily be mistaken as a 'better' sound. Try to keep the processed and bypassed sound at the same level.

> **Tip**
>
> Whether you process using the EQ first or the compression first is a debatable point. You can experiment with both ways and see which works best for you.

Compression

You may want to use compression to 'level' out a completed and mixed song. Many compressors have a 'sound', which they will impose on the songs. Some compression plug-ins simulate valve or classic compressors, which again have their own specific 'sound'.

The problems with compressing a whole track is that one element of the sound, say the bass drum, may trigger the compressor in a way that isn't suitable for the rest of the track. You may find the track 'pumping' or distorting in some way. Gentle compression is usually needed here.

Try these settings as a starting point
- Ratio. Try a compression ratio in the range 2:1 to 5:1
- Attack. Set this to 2ms or fast. This means the signal is affected quickly – i.e.

the compressor works right away to keep sound level in volume.

- Release. Set this to around 0.5s. You'll need to experiment with this value. To slow a release will make the sound unnatural.
- Threshold. Turn down the threshold control until the compressor starts to work (you'll see the gain reduction in the meter on the compressor). Further reduce the control until you get a nice level sound.
- Gain make up. Increases the value of the gain make-up control until the compressed song is at the same level as the non-compressed one.

Multi band compression

One way to get around the problems with 'normal' compression is to use a multi band compressor. These split the audio stream into many frequency bands – usually 3 or 4. The frequency ranges of the bands are variable and each band has its own compressor. The idea behind multi band compressors is that you can affect various frequency ranges in different ways. For example, you could compress the mid range more than the bass, or select a narrow frequency range to correct for excessive sibilance.

Some multi band compressors allow individual threshold levels to be adjusted along with an 'overall' one. You can 'solo' each individual frequency band to hear the effect on that band alone.

Multi band compressors are complex beasts by their very nature and the parameters available may vary. However they usually come with a range of presets to get you started.

Figure 10.6

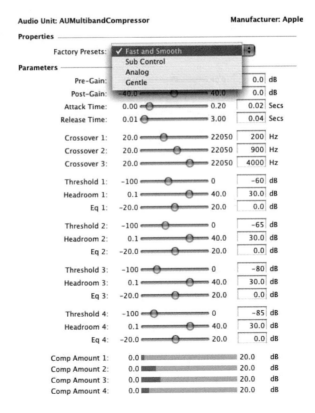

Tip

See Chapter 5 for more on Logic's Multiband compressors.

EQ

Whereas during mixing we were often using EQ (equalisation or tone correction) to correct and enhance individual instruments, when mastering it's a more gentle correction that is required. You may want to subtly enhance the high frequencies or reduce or enhance the bass.

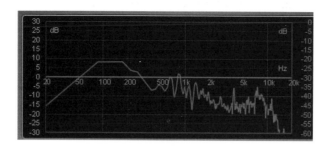

Figure 10.7

Tip

You can use the Multi Meter to display the overall frequency range for a song. This can be extremely useful to see if you have any gross 'bumps' in the frequency range of your song. However, it always best to confirm any analysis by using your ears!

The EQ you use is going to be dependent on the type of Song you are mastering and the result you are trying to get – but here's a few settings to try as a starting point.

*   Boost a few dBs at around 15000Hz to add 'air' to the track – but watch for sibilance.
*   Boost at around 80Hz to enhance the low end. Cut at 300Hz to remove muddiness. Don't be tempted to use too much boost or cut.

Figure 10.8

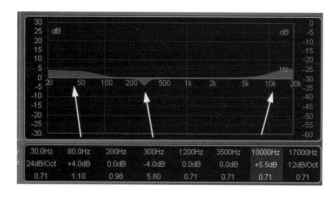

Tip

You may want to use a third-party 'classic' emulation of EQ and/or compression to enhance the overall 'tone' of the mix.

Figure 10.9

Tip

If you find that you are boosting or cutting frequencies by a large amount to make the song sound OK, you should consider re-mixing the song.

Figure 10.10

Limiting or Maximising

Limiting is the last effect you should use in the mastering chain. It's a severe form of compression, which stops the output going over a certain pre-set level. This will allow you to push the level as high as possible without hitting 0dB and digital distortion. In addition, limiters often have the facility to pull up low-level signals, thus compressing the sound into a narrow volume range. These limiters are often called maximisers.

The Ad Limiter is most suitable for mastering. Insert it after the EQ and Compressor and try the following settings as a guide.

- Set the Out ceiling to –0.3 dB. This will stop the level ever going higher than this.
- Set the Input Scale to 0dB
- Set the Gain to 0dB
- Play the Track.

Initially bring up the Gain control to increase apparent loudness. You may have to reduce the gain and increase the Input to get a musically useful result.

Processing all the songs with the same plug-ins and settings

You can use exactly the same plug-ins when processing each channel separately, but you'll put them on the master stereo output instead of each individual track. This means that all the songs will be processed by the same plug-in parameters.

You can of course, use a combination of the two techniques. For example you could have individual EQ and/or compression on each track, but the limiter on the master output only.

Other mastering effects

While the above are the 'classic' mastering effects, you may also like to try some other plug-ins to enhance your songs.

- Logic's Exciter. This is a specialised plug-in that applies EQ, distortion and compression to make the sound more 'present' and brighter in tone. Exciters can initially make things sound very impressive – but may be wearing on the ear after a while, so be careful how you apply them.
- Valve emulators. These plug-ins add a 'warmth' to the sound. Overused, they can make things sound woolly and muddy.

Bouncing down the mix

This is done in exactly the same way as for mixing – except that you need to use 16 bit 44.1KHz as the file format if you are transferring to CD (Figure 10.11). However, as you'll usually be be converting from a higher bit rate and/or sample rate you'll need to 'dither' the audio when you bounce down. Dither is a specialised filtering technique that smoothes out the data and reduces artifacts from the conversion. Logic uses the POW-r dithering algorithm.

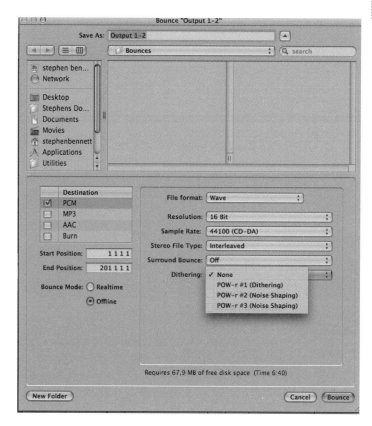

Figure 10.11

POW-r dithering algorithm

Logic's internal resolution is 32 bit floating point. However, you will often bounce down to 24 bit for mastering or 16 bit files for CD creation. Dithering reduces unwanted graininess and quantisation noise produced during this bit reduction. The POW-r algorithm has three types of dithering. Which one you use depends on the source file. As usual, let your ears be the judge. However, some use examples are given below.

- None. No dithering occurs. Use this if you want to re-import audio for mastering or adding to an already recorded track.
- POW-r #1. Uses a dithering curve to reduce noise. Use on acoustic music that has been recorded at a decent level or natural sounding music.
- POW-r #2. Uses noise shaping to add an extra 10dB to the dynamic range. Use on low level recorded acoustic or anywhere you need the added dynamic range.
- POW-r #3. Uses noise shaping to extend the dynamic range by 20dB in the 2 to 4 kHz range. This is the range most sensitive to the human ear. Use on pop, rock or dance music or music destined for the radio. Or voice recordings.

Tip

Dithering should only be performed on the final bounce of before final CD production. If you try to dither already dithered audio, sound quality will suffer.

Figure 10.12

Order of mastering plug-ins

There are some rules about the ordering of the plug-ins on a channel strip for mastering, and some areas of flexibility.

EQ and Compression

Which goes first is a matter of taste. If you use the routing method in Figure 10.12 the EQ cannot compensate for any dulling of the sound caused by the compressor. Also, the EQ frequencies that have been boosted will get compressed more than those that have not.

Of course you could have the routing in Figure 10.13 which may solve that problem! If you use the routing in Figure 10.14 you'll get a different sound, as the EQ won't be affected by peaks in the audio.

Figure 10.13

Figure 10.14

So, here's a suggested order for your mastering plug-ins.

- EQ or Compression (single or multiband)
- Compression or EQ (single or multiband)
- Exciter or valve emulator (if needed)
- Limiter or Maximiser
- Dither (if needed)

Index